1|19

You're Welcome,
CLEVELAND

Also by Scott Raab

The Whore of Akron

You're Welcome,
CLEVELAND

How I Helped LeBron James
Win a Championship
and Save a City

SCOTT RAAB

HARPER

An Imprint of HarperCollins*Publishers*

HarperCollins books may be purchased for educational, business,
or sales promotional use. For information, please email the
Special Markets Department at SPsales@harpercollins.com.

FIRST EDITION

Designed by Bonni Leon-Berman

Library of Congress Cataloging-in-Publication Data has been
applied for.
ISBN 978-0-06-239686-0
17 18 19 20 21   LSC   10 9 8 7 6 5 4 3 2 1

To my father—Sanford Raab—and to
David, Robert, and Michael, my brothers

CONTENTS

You're Welcome, CLEVELAND

1

REVELATION

I'm home again, among my people for Game 7 of the 2016 NBA Finals—in downtown Cleveland, in a bar on Huron Avenue, a two-floor cavern in a century-old bank building that sat vacant for ten years and sold for less than we'll get for our house in New Jersey next year. Every tap in the city is jammed, and in the streets outside, two hundred thousand natives huddle, howling, praying for salvation, beseeching King James.

Poor bastards. The score is 89-89 with two minutes left, and both teams have gone cold, gripped by fatigue and the vise of Game 7. With each missed shot, this saloon swells with body heat and a roar less animal than machine. Fifty years of failure is the sound of hope in my hometown.

I have come to warn my people of the coming flood of tears, but I cannot make a sound, and none of them could hear me anyway, and none of them would listen if they could.

Fools.

Then the Warriors rebound another Cavs miss and start a

textbook two-on-one fast break: Andre Iguodala and Steph Curry, honeyed godling, running hard, splitting the court against the Cavs' rescue adoptee, the dubitable J. R. Smith.

I know what's coming, know it in my bones. Grief and irony, irony and grief, laid atop fifty-two years of loss, and sealed with an enduring fury. My first and last Game 7 was nearly twenty years ago, when the Cleveland Indians took a one-run lead into the ninth inning and blew it. No chariot came; no chariot has come since. I am among the living who saw the Browns win it all in 1964, when I was twelve. I was baptized in the spirit of Jim Brown then, on the Lake Erie shore, but I have seen the town and these teams crumble and collapse for fifty years, and my heart is a scar hard with dread and despair, and my faith consists of duty, not belief.

At the midcourt line, Iguodala passes to Curry, who swings wide, to draw JR out of Iguodala's way. One step, and Curry zips the ball back, a bounce pass that Iguodala catches in stride as he arrows to the hoop. JR has recovered and curls past just as Iguodala jumps, the ball aloft in his right hand. JR has done his best; he always does, to little avail.

This can't end well—and it won't be the team's fault, much less this woebegone town's. Blame this old Jew, wandering parched in endless, empty sands, cursing at the faceless sky. Not a prophet: a dollar-store Virgil trembling at hell's gate. A curse incarnate.

My son is here, only seventeen years old, still saddled with me. I've heard that dads hunt and fish and camp. Dads golf. Dads build things—often using power tools—and dads somehow repair them. Not my dad. Not me. I hit the road with Judah and drive through the night to my hometown, so that we might bear witness to another Cleveland team turn triumph into a rictus of defeat and misery.

Judah, my beloved heir, here is my gift, your legacy: Game 7 in the land of your fathers, and a soul-crushing defeat—on Father's Day.

AND AS THE BALL leaves Iguodala's hand, LeBron, out of the ether, streaks into the paint. For eighty-eight feet, nearly the entire length of the court, he has sprinted behind the play, seeing all of it during the three or four seconds since the rebound.

Trailing Iguodala by two yards, he launches, at the perfect angle and instant, soaring toward the ball, still rising, his hands held high, arms spread, carrying the weight of a people and a city's soul.

A foot above the rim, LeBron James blocks the shot and cracks the sky.

I CAN'T BELIEVE MY eyes, which are brimming with what could be tears of joy, though I don't believe for a moment that the Cavaliers are actually going to win this game. There's too much time left, the score's still tied, and twenty thousand fans in Oracle Arena, three thousand miles away in Oakland, are standing: Fops, arrogant, soft, with cash to burn. Heartless, greedy, demanding glory as their due, cheering for their defending champs, who have won more regular-season games than any team in NBA history, and for the first-ever unanimous MVP, Steph, sweetheart of the hardwood.

The Warriors and Cavs trade misses for a minute on the clock, time enough to lock eyes with my son, mine only child, New Jersey born and bred. His gray eyes shine. He is a pale prince, lean, quick, strong. He gets his sinew and good foot speed from the Brennans—my wife's side. From my side, he gets warnings and wisecracking.

I don't know what he sees when he looks at me. I am sixty-three, thick, slow, bummy enough to be too often mistaken for his grandfather, stamped in the image of Sanford Raab, my father, who died eleven days ago, early on June 8—or, as I'll always think of it, Game 3.

The Cavs curb-stomped Golden State that night, rose to their knees after losing badly in the first two games of the Finals. I can't credit Sandy. He was no Cavaliers fan—he lived most of his life, and died, in Los Angeles, and boxing was his only sports obsession—but he, too, walked these streets when he was twenty and thirty. He isn't here—my brother Michael in Burbank has the cremains—but I am, and so is Judah Raab.

WITH FIFTY-THREE SECONDS LEFT, Kyrie Irving launches a step-back rainbow inches over Curry's fingertips, a rainbow that kisses the far rim and whirls through the net, and the Cavs go up 92-89.

I'm still in doubt of everything but doom. This is not possible: no team in NBA history has come back to win the title after being down three games to one. I left the Cavaliers for dead then, a week ago, after Game 4. Bled of belief, unready for joy, insufferable to myself, I kept driving us, dodging deer on I-80 for nine hundred miles round-trip, driven by the same primitive force that led me to pay the mohel to mutilate my eight-day-old son: a covenant of myth.

Now—NOW—the answer is at hand to the fundamental question: Does the God of Sports loathe Cleveland even more than Yahweh hates His Chosen People?

This can't happen—not against the Warriors in Game 7, not in Cleveland, not on Father's Day. Of all the bitter, burning losses over half a century, this would be the worst by far. I will survive it—my whole life has steeled me for this—and someday, surely, Judah will bounce back.

ONLY IN THE ASTONISHMENT that follows—Kevin Love locks down Steph Curry at the three-point line, a sentence no more likely than "Babe Ruth died a virgin"—does doubt creep into my doubt. Love, Cleveland's gentle Billy Budd, is all of a sudden a dervish, and Curry, smothered, befuddled, heaves another hopeless cinder block.

Miss.

Cavs' ball.

With ten seconds left, LeBron goes down hard at the other

end, fouled at the Warriors basket by Draymond Green, a gift box of jewels wrapped in razor wire. It was a clean shot—rare for Draymond in these playoffs, where his various assaults on opponents' junk have already cost him a Finals game suspension—but LeBron lands on his right shoulder and wrist, and down he stays, writhing on the floor as if torn at by wolves.

The entire Cavs' bench—players, coaches, assistants, and trainer—jog down to surround and console him. Finally, he is able to stand.

Ecce LeBron. His battered majesty. His body hewn of boulders from Olympus. Two free throws ice the game.

Two free throws.

He botches the first, rattles home the second.

93-89.

In order of their likelihood, three possibilities remain: a Cavalier foul on a three-point Warrior make, after which the single free throw for the foul knots the game, forcing overtime and killing me outright; or a tsunami swallows Oracle; or this is the best night of my life, and Cleveland's.

Build the ark, man. Build the fucking ark. Now.

Too late. Curry clanks his final three, and as LeBron waves his teammates away from the ball, the game clock runs out.

It is finished.

LeBron has brought his people home, turned our home into the Promised Land, and I'm alive, in Cleveland, weeping, waltzing with my boy.

EVERYONE POURS OUT INTO the street, except us. I have a plan. I always have a plan. When I was young, I had weapons. Now I am no longer young, and my son is not yet grown. I love Cleveland; I don't trust it, not tonight. What may come when the tectonics of passion erupt at the hour of liberation from fifty-two years of misery—from folks who've spent two generations in abjection, plus all day and half the night pounding beer—who knows? Besides, we fly at six a.m. to Newark: Judah, an eleventh-grader, has two quarterly exams.

So we take the back stairs to the alley, piss, and work ourselves back to the hotel. East Ninth Street is bedlam. A fire truck sails past, fans dangling from its length like pirates from a mast. We walk north, toward the lake, then west on Short Vincent, shadowed by the gangster Jews of yore— Mushy Wexler, Shondor Birns, names my son has never heard—then tack north and west to Superior Avenue.

The moon is full and Cleveland's lit. I never dreamed this Capra fantasy. Twenty times in a block we hug fans streaming back to the street party we left behind. I'm so ecstatic, I can't even feel my bad hip. Two police officers stand guard at the front of the old library, across from our hotel, with not a thing to do but smile and wave at the cars honking by.

In the room, we flip from the local news to ESPN and back. We fly at six, but all I want to do is watch the block again, on an infinite loop.

Sitting alone at the interview podium, J. R. Smith can

barely speak for weeping. His father, Earl, stands against one wall.

"My dad put the ball in my crib," JR says, and buries his head in his hands. When he raises it again, the tears are still streaming and his voice is breaking.

"I've been in a lot of dark spots in my life. My parents, my family, they fought with me, they yelled at me, they loved me, they hugged me, they cried with me, and they always stuck by my side."

I'm trying to keep from crying too loud. I look over to the kid. Sound asleep. In four hours, he'll be on the plane with his history book spread on the tray and a cup of black coffee in his hand. He'll go from Newark airport straight to school and bang out two more A's. Senior year next year and he's gone. He'll be taking his talents to wherever-the-fuck.

It hits me only now: this, tonight, was our last shot.

Thank you, LeBron.

LEBRON'S AT THE PODIUM now, his baby girl on his lap and his two sons flanking him. A net, fresh cut from Oracle Arena's baskets, is draped around his neck.

"I came back to bring a championship to our city," King James says. "I'm coming home with what I said I was going to do. I'm coming home."

APOLOGIA

If I went too far when LeBron James left Cleveland for Miami back in 2010, it's not for me to judge. I didn't burn his jersey—I didn't have one. But Judah did, and I told him to toss it in the trash rather than burn it—fires scare me. He was eleven years old then, and already he had seen all of his favorite players, each and every one, depart Cleveland. Now LeBron.

I had no T-shirt. No ring. No words of hope to tell my son.

What I had was a book to write. I'd spent that season, 2009–2010, following the team, credentialed by the Cavs. It was LeBron's walk year, and GM Danny Ferry and coach Mike Brown were also in the final year of their contracts. Last season's team had won 66 games, tops in the league, the year before, but lost to Orlando in the Eastern Conference Finals. Now it was win or else.

There were portents from the start. On draft day, the Cavaliers signed the aged Shaquille O'Neal, and Michael Jackson died. Also Farrah Fawcett. Then the Cavs drafted

Christian Eyenga, a twenty-year-old from Kinshasa—nobody in the press room had ever heard of him—and Danny Green, whose name, thanks to Cleveland's legendary crime boss, the Irishman, Danny Greene, was greeted with chuckles from the old-timers in the media room.

The season ended with Game 5 against Boston in the second round of the 2010 playoffs. The Cavs were heavy favorites, but the series was tied at two wins apiece when LeBron had a horrid game, at home. He wandered as if entranced, hit three of fourteen shots, was booed off the court as the Celtics won by thirty-two, 120-88. It was a scourging loss. At the postgame press conference afterward, LeBron seemed as bitter and angry as the fans.

"I spoil a lot of people with my play," he said at one point.

It ended two nights later, in Boston, in Game 6. On the final night of his seventh season in the wine and gold, LeBron ripped off his jersey on his way through the tunnel and flung it away.

On July 8, 2010, LeBron took an hour of prime time to announce that he was leaving Cleveland for Miami. I was far from the only idiot who felt personally betrayed.

Having straddled half a century of Cleveland sports like a bear at stool, I went large. I used The Decision to frame and vent decades of misery, Cleveland's pain and my own, and I damned a young baller—a young African American man who came up hard in West Akron—for the sin of not being my Moses, and called the book *The Whore of Akron*.

JESUS. WHAT AN ASSHOLE. But what the hell: I at least wanted my words to leave a mark. I knew he had every right to leave, to make the call about what was best for him and his family. I myself left Cleveland in 1984, to go to writing school. Nobody offered me $100 million to stay put—my last job in Cleveland was as a nursing-home night watchman—and the hopes and dreams of a nation of fans weren't dashed when my first wife and I stuffed our shit into a U-Haul, drugged the cats, and hit I-80 to Iowa City. I don't recall spending an hour on ESPN nut-punching my hometown. And to this day, I doubt that I could haul down twenty grand as a writer working in Cleveland. He was the Chosen One, not me, a native son who'd spent seven seasons saying he felt our pain and wouldn't go chasing rings. Then he did.

I watched The Decision, saw that young putz in his checkered shirt reveal his treachery to Jim Gray, withered crone; saw Cleveland trashed again, on national TV; saw the burning jerseys and the cops patrolling underneath the regal banner lest the hordes descend with torches and pitchforks.

No hordes, not in Cleveland or New Jersey. I sat with my wife, seething the entire hour, blood curdled, outraged, and when my boy came home from the mean streets of Glen Ridge, I delivered him the news.

"Fuck LeBron," Judah said.

O noble son! Delectable fruit of my loins! It took me back to one of his first sentences, spoken in Strasburg, Pennsylvania, when steam locomotives, not Cleveland sports, were his mother's milk. He spotted an SUV in a restaurant parking lot, adorned with a New York Yankees spare tire cover on its ass.

"Fuck Derek Jeter," he said.

My son took no pleasure tossing his wine-and-gold LeBron jersey into the kitchen trash. I took no pride in it. The greatest player I had ever seen was gone, and fury, cold or hot, felt foolish, weak. Yet it had to be done. I had advised Judah long before that he could and should find his own, non-Cleveland teams to worship and adore—as long as it wasn't the fucking Yankees—and I believed that I believed that. But when I held him for the first time, sprung from the womb, eyes lit by the world, cradled by the racist visage of Chief Wahoo tattooed on my arm—from that day hence, he was a member of the tribe.

No man is truly author of his fate: no son, no father, not even LeBron James, who left town trailing Cleveland from his Nikes like a smear of dog shit, headed for South Beach.

I alone was left to tell the tale.

I DID THINGS NO so-called journalist would do. I motherfucked him on Twitter. For the Heat's first trip to Cleveland, I offered $500 to the Cavs' media VP to let me stand between LeBron and the chalk he'd toss pregame. For the Heat's next Cleveland visit, I shaved my head and scrawled QUITNESS thick and red on my skull.

All this came quite naturally to me—I'd been a thuggish

fan since my midteens—but I didn't skimp on the reporting. I stayed in Miami for a week or two at a time during Heat home stands, going to games—the team had yanked my credentials, so I bought tickets—and trying to understand why in the world anyone in his right mind, especially a young, wealthy icon and a man of color, would abandon Akron and Cleveland for Miami.

I learned exactly why—I couldn't resist Miami despite its warmth and beauty—and this, like LeBron's excellence, only fueled my rage. Hunkered down in Cleveland for much of the season, I watched my team and my hometown gutted, bleeding out.

Had LeBron left behind a championship banner, I would've bid him farewell with more gratitude than sadness. The only questions lingering would've been where and when to plant his statue.

No ring, no statues. Instead, he fled to Miami cackling about how easy winning titles would be now that he was not a Cavalier—not three rings, not four, not five—counting them out to the roar of his new, sun-addled subjects.

It was a long and ugly season. I stuck it out to the end, in Miami's arena, cheering as LeBron fell apart and the Heat lost the NBA Finals to the Dallas Mavericks. It felt good for an hour or two, and then it struck me that Cleveland fanhood had reduced me to an impoverishment so ghastly that the only pleasure I could take was in someone else's woe.

I wrote the book that I was born to write. I wrote about his *schmeckle*, I wrote about his mom, I wrote "FUCK LEBRON"

in block capitals above my name when I signed copies—
though I signed the copy I left with the sentry at his mansion
gate, "Thanks for making this book possible."

I went as hard and as long as an old kike at the keyboard
can go, because that's what Cleveland taught me. Had we
stepped onto the court, with cash on the line and one basketball, what respect or mercy would LeBron have offered me?

3
PRODIGAL

It hurt to watch him win two rings with the Heat, but I watched. I had to watch. I had earned a good living as a magazine writer years before LeBron snagged his first Nike deal—five years with *GQ* in the mid-1990s, then nineteen years at *Esquire*— and I'd written plenty about notorious Clevelanders: Dennis Kucinich and Don King, Kevin Mackey and John Demjanjuk, Paul Assenmacher and Sanford Raab—and now I was a pox upon LeBron. I rode with that, too. Sports talk radio. Mending fences with ESPN, after I'd ripped them hard in the book. Hustling. Always closing. You can count on blind luck and white privilege for only so much and so long, and I was already sixty years old. So I kept going hard, hard as a motherfucker.

LeBron stepped it up, too. Shocked to find himself booed in every NBA arena every time he touched the ball during his first Heat season, he turned cold. He played without expression, frowning even on his best nights. Judah and I watched him drop fifty-one points on Orlando in a meaningless February game and never even grin.

"He's hard to hate," the kid said on his way upstairs to bed.

Nah. A couple of weeks before, as the husk of the Cavaliers soiled themselves against the Lakers, losing by an otherworldly score of 112-57—Christian Eyenga notched four points in seven minutes off the bench—LeBron threw up a "Karma is a bitch" tweet. Fucker.

The Heat's loss to the Mavericks in the Finals drove him deep into himself. He talked about what it cost him to embrace anger as a mind-set. He spoke of rediscovering his love of the game and the joy it gave back to him. He even admitted fault for turning The Decision into a sixty-minute enema.

"I'm not here to ask for any sympathy or apologies," LeBron said. "Win, lose, or draw, I'm playing because I'm grateful that I'm a kid from Akron, Ohio, that made it to the NBA, that made his dream a reality. That's what I'm happy about, so I can't take it for granted."

Whoa. Twenty-seven years old, in the prime of his prime, and he's growing wise in spirit, too? At his age, I was dealing weed in Austin, Texas, writing poetry. LeBron led the Heat to the NBA Championship in his second season in Miami, and won again in his third. I wrote one good villanelle and left Texas in a hurry, owing money I didn't have.

What had taken me decades—literally thousands of hours of therapy, years of sobriety, a divorce—this young fellow had dealt with in his off-season. He had accepted the loss and hurt as part of him, tasted loss, bitterness, and anger, and then went back to work with gratitude and joy.

Motherfucker. I bought a treadmill, set it up where I could see the TV, and started walking every day. I started a food journal—no feelings, just a list of everything I ate. I had topped out at 380 pounds and blown out a lower-back disk while working on *The Whore*, and I was still way past three bills when the treadmill came. By the time LeBron won his first ring, I'd dropped a hundred pounds. The back was better. Sex was better. I felt better.

Life was good, very good. All the misery—ALL of it—was confined to Cleveland sports. I understood that now, thank G-d: I would never again see a Cleveland team win a championship. Fine. Maybe Judah, *kinehora*, would. I'm good. Just bless my boy.

HE COMES HOME. He comes home because the Heat failed to three-peat, and he comes home because the happy wife makes possible a happy life, and Savannah Brinson James is pregnant with their third child and she misses Akron. He comes home to help raise their kids in a place far safer and saner—and cheaper; LeBron pinches pennies—than Miami. He comes home because he'll have far more leverage over the Cavaliers than Pat Riley ever let him wield with the Heat. He comes home because he envisions Kyrie Irving as a sidekick who will share some of the pressure. He comes home because, while no man is truly author of his fate, a guy sometimes must set the bush on fire himself. A hero needs a quest.

LeBron's homecoming essay in *Sports Illustrated* broke me like a wafer. After a lifetime telling stories, I know bullshit when I smell it, and there's not a false word in that paean to work, love, and the grip a boy's home holds forever on a grown man's heart. Lee Jenkins, the writer, gave structure and flow to those words. I know and admire Jenkins's work, and so do LeBron and his people. They sat, LeBron and his crew with the writer, and LeBron drank tea, chamomile no doubt, and talked it out for hours.

That's LeBron's voice, saying exactly what Cleveland fans wanted and needed to hear: he was coming back, to humbly seek—no party, press conference, or promise—a crown for Cleveland.

But there was more, and Lee Jenkins didn't conjure it.

"I feel my calling here goes above basketball. I have a responsibility to lead, in more ways than one, and I take that very seriously. My presence can make a difference in Miami, but I think it can mean more where I'm from. I want kids in Northeast Ohio, like the hundreds of Akron third-graders I sponsor through my foundation, to realize that there's no better place to grow up. Maybe some of them will come home after college and start a family or open a business. That would make me smile. Our community, which has struggled so much, needs all the talent it can get."

Okay, so the "hundreds of Akron third-graders" clause is a clunker. But those kids exist, no less vital to the world than my son, living in greater need by far. He had guaranteed them tuition at the University of Akron if they stayed true to their promise to him—to work at their studies. He wasn't just coming home big; he'd lift the suffering of his people AND deliver fans from fifty years of bondage.

"I'm ready to accept the challenge," LeBron said. "I'm coming home."

Amen. And, hallelujah.

I'M NOT SAYING LEBRON read *The Whore of Akron*, or Homer, or the Bible. I'm not sneering, either. I'm just saying that nobody has ever pimped a hero narrative as full of redemption's nectar as Nike and Wieden+Kennedy. The Return of LeBron to The Land is impossible not to parse—with admiration—as a mythic rebranding, perfectly conceived, flawlessly executed.

I'm also saying that LeBron's return meant far more than an operatic shoe ad for forlorn Cleveland, itself a quest in aching need of a hero. Here he was, four years gone, his brow etched, his hairline heading due north, still somehow not yet thirty years of age, married to an Akron sweetheart from his high school, the father of two sons, with a daughter on the way, trying to live his one life right.

He had become a global spokesman, a brand unto himself, a hardwood auteur, a boardroom *macher*, a global icon. He embodied more than the face of the NBA: LeBron's escape from Cleveland had mapped a new route to freedom for every star in the league; and he spoke of his colleagues as one brotherhood when the racism of LA Clippers owner Donald Sterling was expunged; and he stood with his Miami teammates—heads down and hooded—after Trayvon Martin was shot dead for being young and black.

That consciousness mattered. Beyond basketball, beyond commerce, beyond Akron and Cleveland, it spoke to bigger, crucial scars and seeping wounds. LeBron had lived his life as a product and a cultural projection. He was Judah's age when *Sports Illustrated* put him on its cover and called him the Chosen One—and now that kid was coming home enrobed in glory, lightning in his hands, full Moses.

I READ THE ESSAY with joy, embarrassment, and shame. No man is truly author of his fate, but I was the author of *The Whore of Akron.*

I was also the sad sack who still clung to his ticket stub from that 1964 NFL Championship game, and who knew this was the best day in Cleveland, sports or no, since 1964. It meant more than a lift to Cleveland's spirit and economy, more even than another book for Raab, a Norman Mailer fan.

All that mattered to Raab was that the Cavaliers would once again put the best player in the league out on the court every night. Cleveland had a chance—my son and I included—at a championship, a shot at immortality.

Judah was playing pickup soccer at the park. I texted him the news; he knew, of course.

Then the calls rolled in from ESPN, CNN, and radio guys, all wanting the whore who wrote *The Whore* to offer his commentary on LeBron's return.

I told the truth: He left Cleveland as the best player in the league—the best basketball player I've ever seen—and he got even better with the Heat. He won two chips, plus Olympic gold. Beyond a doubt, he proved that leaving Cleveland was the right call. All he did wrong—all LeBron has EVER done wrong, besides undertip—was to exercise his right of free agency in a manner I deemed ungracious.

My bad.

What else was there to say, and, by the way, who gives a damn?

King James is coming back.

"Who am I to hold a grudge?" he and Lee Jenkins asked.

Me too, *Mashiach*. Me too. I wouldn't rewrite *The Whore* if I could, but I wronged you and I'm sorry. I went too far, blurred some lines dividing sanity and lunacy—not to mention love and hate—but nobody got hurt, and between you and me, that besotted free fall into mania and pure id—for a certain kind of fan, or a certain kind of writer—throbs like ecstasy itself. Well-adjusted men don't choose zealotry or writing; men with loose screws do.

THE KID COMES HOME after soccer and I meet him at the door. He's shining. I'm a mess. I need a hug.

"You've been crying all this time?"

On and off. I had to do some radio.

He laughs. I want him to laugh when I cry. My father's father ditched my dad when he was twelve—walked out and never came home again. My father abandoned me when I was ten—he fell in love with a coworker after he moved us to Los Angeles when I was eight, and let my mother flee with us back to her parents' house in Cleveland. I saw him cry once, almost, when he showed up in his rental car on his yearly trip to see us, and my coldhearted mother ordered me to get into the car and dun him for stiffing her on the child support. I got in his car and spoke my piece, and saw his shoulders slump and heave. I can't see his face, or hear anything he said. I don't know if he spoke. I don't remember sobbing. My shame, hurt, and anger I do recall.

I want my son to see me cry with happiness, shamelessly. I grew up in an Orthodox household headed by old Slovakian trash—a pensioned railroad laborer and a bakery clerk, my grandparents. Short version: I came of age fatherless, fat, and furious—tattoos and guns, rage and wine and pills. I wasn't Charles Bukowski or John Fante or Harvey Pekar: I was the Nigger of the Ashkenazi. I should have been in jail or dead, or broke down like my old man. Instead, I wake up here, drenched in milk and honey.

LeBron is coming home, and I'm crying, and Judah laughs at me and hugs me so hard I feel my back crack. *Kinehora.*

You see the essay?

"What essay?"

If you want a fucking jersey, you gotta read the fucking essay.

"Nah. I'm good."

4
MEDIA DAY 2014

Essay or no essay, somebody's holding a grudge. The Cavaliers deny my application for credentials on Media Day. I e-mailed a note along with the request; I knew that it would be tricky. Maybe LeBron and his partners—I had dropped off a second copy of the first book at their office in downtown Cleveland—didn't know it, but they knew the title and the hashtag. His agent had blocked me on Twitter.

"There is history that we need to consider, and numerous segments of it are difficult for us to reconcile and translate into access moving forward," Tad Carper, the team's media VP, wrote me.

Segments, shmegments. Tad and Dan Gilbert "were under the impression" that I'd provide advance copy that included any of Dan's "quotes, attributions, and recollections," one of the very few things that separate journalism from public relations—and something I've neither promised nor given to any subject or source in my career.

I refused. Instead, I dropped off advance copies of the book—and I was greeted like a cousin, welcome anytime.

It stayed that way until LeBron came home. Believe me, I understood. I'd spoken to him only twice during his last season in Cleveland—he stopped talking to the media during his free-agent year—first because I needed a quote for a Shaq profile, and then after the Cavs' last regular-season home game, to tell him he was the best basketball player I'd even seen.

It's Media Day, Tad. The King is back. Hundreds of journalists. Nobody will even know I'm polluting the facility.

No. "After additional consideration of your request, we are going to decline. We do wish you the best and would love to watch you celebrate a Cavs championship and read your personal account of it."

My final offer: Media Day, and nothing else, except maybe a postseason interview with Dan.

Tad refuses.

My final final offer: I'll bring the donuts.

Tad declines.

This is serious now.

I reach out to Dan Gilbert. His wife and mine had talked property taxes at a Nets game in Newark in 2012; he'd shown me a Bar Mitzvah video he'd produced for his son—a lavish parody of The Decision—and Dan told Tad to tell me to fuck off. In truth, he didn't put it that way. Tad told me if LeBron or his people—LeBron came with people—knew I was nosing around, there'd be trouble.

Dan Gilbert, whose Comic Sans runaway-slave letter after The Decision made *The Whore of Akron* look like a Disneyland postcard, was forgiven. James Blair, a young lout who'd run out on the court to hug LeBron during a Heat-Cavs game and had been hauled to the pokey and barred for life from the arena, was forgiven.

I and I alone had gone too far.

THREE HUNDRED JOURNALISTS FROM around the globe come to Media Day, so many that the team's running a shuttle bus to the practice facility from a steakhouse parking lot nearby. LeBron is remounting his throne, and the world is watching. It's Rosh Hashanah, 5775.

I'm at the bus stop, in the steakhouse parking lot, handing out donuts to my media nieces and nephews as they wait for a lift to the coronation. They're kind enough to say that they are sorry I have no credential, that it's unfair.

I don't need no stinking credential. I have sinkers. *L'shana Tovah!*

LeBron has come back home, and so have I. As for fair, it's good to be the guy who brings the donuts. My concern isn't what passes for official access—I still have a few teeth left in my head, and a few friends around town—I'm worried about LeBron's weight loss. Seriously.

LeBron's listed height and weight—6′8″, 250—hasn't changed since he came into the league as an eighteen-year-old. In real life, he's 6′9″, and his playing weight has been in the 265–275 range for years. This summer, he spent nine weeks on a ketogenic Paleo diet—nothing but protein, vegetables, and low-starch fruit—and dropped twenty-five pounds.

"Every summer, I challenge myself to do something that's outside the box," he tells the credentialed media. "I decided to do this particular diet this summer. It had nothing to do with basketball. I can still fly above the rim—I don't need to lose weight to do that. Once I set a goal, I like to accomplish it. In the process, I lost some weight."

I don't know. In the photos he Instagrammed in August, he looks like a big kickboxer. His stomach is carved, but his shoulders have shrunk. His face is thin. *Schlecht.* It's more disturbing than the photo parade depicting the champagne- and coke-infused summer of Johnny Mayfly, the Browns' first-round rookie quarterback. Manziel is already a folk hero among the more bucket-headed Browns fans, few of whom have ever paid close attention to a decent NFL team, none of whom will live to see him become a competent pro QB.

LeBron had better not be ill. The Clevelandest thing ever would be King James coming home now and dropping dead.

THE CAVS HAVE HAD a busier summer, of necessity. When LeBron left in 2010, they embarked on the worst rebuilding job imaginable. They fired a bad coach, Mike Brown, and hired a worse coach, Byron Scott. With an array of lottery picks, including two separate shots at the first pick overall, they picked Kyrie and crapola, while the cheap free agents fizzled briefly and left. After three horrible seasons, they canned Byron Scott, and in a masterstroke of pure ADD, rehired Mike Brown.

In February, Dan Gilbert finally fired the buffoon who oversaw this entire demolition derby, and the new buffoon fired Mike Brown in May and, after eight weeks of searching, hired David Blatt, fifty-five years old, whose undergraduate thesis at Princeton examined the fiction of Bernard Malamud.

Blatt had also played point guard at Princeton, learning the game from the legendary Princeton coach and offensive guru Pete Carril. (And if I mention Princeton once more, maybe they'll let Judah in.)

After Princeton, Blatt went to Israel to play, and when he was through playing, he became a coach. Israel, Greece, Turkey, Russia: everywhere Blatt went, Blatt won. NBA coaches visited to glean his wisdom, and word was that Golden State's rookie head coach, Steve Kerr, wanted to hire Blatt to be an assistant coach, which would've been Blatt's first NBA job.

The Cavaliers made sure that didn't happen by offering Blatt a three-year, $10 million contract for his very first NBA job ever, as head coach of the Cleveland Cavaliers. A week later, with another first-overall pick, the Cavaliers selected Andrew Wiggins, a nineteen-year-old swingman of great promise. Then Kyrie Irving, sloe-eyed killer, signed a new max deal early in July. A core of raw young talent, a rookie head coach with zero experience in the league, and Cleveland: What could go wrong?

What went wrong was that no one in the Cavs organization had any clue that LeBron wanted to come home. Nine days after drafting Wiggins, two weeks after hiring Blatt, Dan Gilbert flew to Miami, one day after LeBron's people first got in touch with Lee Jenkins. Gilbert apologized for The Letter—which I myself had vocally admired, and which was still up on the team's website—and they closed the deal.

BY THE TIME MEDIA DAY arrived in late September, the Cavs had revamped their roster to fit LeBron. He wanted known and trusted teammates, old heads, veterans who had won rings and could help bind and lift a locker room full of young players already used to losing easy. The Cavs signed two of his Heat running buddies, James Jones and Mike Miller, plus Shawn Marion, who'd played on the Dallas team that ended LeBron's first season in Miami. Their combined age was 104, and they were shot to hell, especially Miller, battered by fourteen NBA seasons. But they also were battle-tested, full-grown men.

If their signings were construed as proof that LeBron now had leverage beyond any player in any sport ever, it was not for nothing. But credit the new buffoon, general manager David Griffin, for quick-stepping Andrew Wiggins off to Minnesota in exchange for Kevin Love, a milky, fragile young power forward with more finesse than muscle, but with scoring and rebounding skills so refined that, at twenty-five, he was already considered among the top ten players in the NBA.

Love's six seasons in Minnesota had been fruitless—often injured, he'd never sniffed the playoffs, and the Timberwolves' front office refused to offer him a max contract. David Griffin had chased him before LeBron's return, but so had many others—Golden State included.

The Wolves wanted Klay Thompson from the Warriors in return for Love, and asked for Andrew Wiggins from the Cavs, but no deal was struck until LeBron came back home. He and Love had won gold medals together in the 2012 Olympics, and it wasn't a tough sell.

The Cavs gladly tossed in Poor Anthony Bennett, 2013's first-overall pick, a player on whom future basketball historians will look back and collapse with laughter, and Love was a Cav.

LeBron was well pleased.

"I don't really care about the twenty-six [points] and twelve [rebounds]. I care about the basketball IQ. His basketball IQ is very, very high. He's a great piece."

Christ, yes. Cleveland now has a Big Three, led by the best ever.

Next year in Jerusalem is now.

5

GETHSEMANE

I had a busy summer, too. On the day of LeBron's scholarship announcement, I meet Taylor Swift for breakfast in New York City. Nice kid. Healthy appetite. Two bodyguards.

I also profile the Browns' then-new head coach, whatever his name was, and I am blessed to see Johnny Manziel's debut as a sad party clown. When I meet the then new guy—whose only previous head coach job had been at the high-school level—I show him my ticket stub from 1964.

"Huh," he says. "Eight dollars."

Thanks to LeBron's return and my own mysterious appeal, I also sign a deal with ESPN—on-air, on-call duty as the Cleveland Guy—and visit with Izzy the Tailor, address on request, who measures me for television suits, quality and very reasonable.

Then I swap my ten-year-old Accord coupe—a six-speed, six-cylinder, bright-red cyclone—for an old-man-grayish Accord hybrid sedan, ideal for I-80 and for Judah when he gets his license. I rent a bedroom in a condo owned by a favorite media nephew—I refuse to shame any of them by name—buy a coffeemaker, and dig in.

I FIRST WITNESS LEBRON as a Cav back in the flesh at the annual preseason Wine & Gold Scrimmage, an intrasquad showcase the Cavs rotate among area colleges. Fans come with their kids—it's usually an afternoon event, free of charge, with a few thousand folks there to cheer. But this is the Return of the King to the Land, Roll Away the Stone Night at Quicken Loans Arena, the House the Taxpayers Built and Maintain with Additional Funds Derived from Subprime Loans and the Casino Nearby, Also Owned by Dan Gilbert.

Admission is free, but you must go online for tickets, and all 20,562 of them are gone in a minute. I snag a pair. Judah demurs—he'd miss two days of school, fine with me but not him, so I ask a Cleveland blogger-podcaster to join me, because—like LeBron—I am a river to my people, and because it's lonesome at ball games by myself.

The place is crazier than the fans. In the seasons since *The Whore of Akron*, I had put behind me the Q's version of what marketers call the "in-game experience"; in this case, a relentless fusillade of aural bullshit, cheap T-shirts, and idiotic time-out contests.

It is worse than I recall. The Cavaliers' payroll now supports two mascots—a human cavorting in a dog costume and another human staggering inside a rig designed as a cartoon tribute to the noble swordsman of the Cavs' original 1970 logo, to whom this gape-mouthed, stone-eyed, staggering macrocephalus bears no likeness. There is a DJ, of course, and a master of ceremonies keening *CLEEEEEEEEEveland* on and off for three hours, and constantly shilling, because every surface and activity in the arena is sponsored, monetized, and force-fed to the unlucky saps who paid to watch a basketball game.

But wait—there is also a squadron of female cheerleaders, bare bellied, bouffed, cleavage squeezed, Spanxed into sequins and hoofing it for cab fare home, and a separate but far more than equal platoon of "street" dancers, young men and women using names like Shogun, Ritz, and Achilles, collectively known as the Scream Team.

Both dance groups can be booked for corporate events, and both remind me that the human condition, even under the kindest circumstances, tends toward the foolish. This comforts me until I remember that I myself have traveled far to fall at LeBron's feet—he can't be back until I see him back—and that at least the dancing fools are burning calories. In the week since Media Day, I have gorged on Cleveland—Seti's Polish Boys; Corky & Lenny's; Melt, grilled cheese's mecca; the hummus at Tommy's on Coventry; Geraci's sausage pizza; Kobe beef corn dogs at Flip Side in Chagrin Falls; and Slyman's, always Slyman's, whose pastrami Reuben is my madeleine.

The Brook Park Recreation Center and its treadmills sit five minutes from the condo, but the only exercise I've had this week is typing—and pecking like a schmuck at Dan Gilbert's slot machines. If all of them are fools, then what am I?

Ah. I am a simple pilgrim. When the lights go down, and the spotlights start to sweep across the floor, and the macrocephalus is revealed, standing center court, I'm on my feet with everybody else, in banshee abandon. Some speak in tongues; some merely wail; some stand and sway, eyes wide, dumbstruck, I among them, deafened now, nodding fast in silent delirium.

He is coming.

He is the last Cav to be introduced, of course. LeBron lopes into the light, haloed by his white headband, slapping hands with his cordoned teammates, impervious to the roar, placid. They huddle up around LeBron for a few seconds and then begin the layup lines.

The noise has banked, but I see no one sitting. We stand rapt, staring in belief. LeBron is home.

He looks a little thin.

MY GOD IS NO HERO—in truth, I'm beginning to think that He's not even God—and my hero is no god. I'm not insane. Because no man is truly author of his fate—or we would never die—we need some rationale, an explanation of our lives and death, a bedtime story. We need a hero, an entity less powerless than us. Apparently I choose to call my Higher Power LeBron.

The need for such nonsense has been true of all men everywhere, Cleveland included. It starts with sentience, with Juno and Hera, Ma and Pa, and with an animism unfettered by doubt until we grow, and the world becomes real, and we can feed no more on blind faith. We go on living in certain knowledge of our doom—numbed with terror literal, absolute, beyond abstraction, seeking peace in tribal myth, comfort in campfire songs, inspiration in art, and passion and truth everywhere. Poor bastards. Juno and Hera turn into Sanford and Lucille Raab—Hi, Mom!—and all the myths and songs, and art itself, inspire fealty and division, passion and truth animate endless tribal warring, and always in the name of whichever Creator is momentarily master of the abattoir.

It's all a trap. Give me Cleveland. Give me LeBron—with or without a championship. If the forty million bucks in scholarships was insufficient, and two books, then seeing him again wearing the colors of my team is truth enough for me. I'm glad to live through him once more, to lose myself in hopeless hope of triumph.

As LeBron has forgiven, we forgive. He has redeemed himself and us, all of us but one.

6
YOM KIPPUR

It's 448 miles direct from the Q to my driveway in New Jersey, 311 of them through Pennsylvania, on Interstate 80. I don't often drive it by night these days. My eyes have dimmed, my reactions have slowed, and I'm not in a hurry. Yom Kippur starts at sunset the day after tomorrow; I have time. And it's deer season, when I-80 abounds with grim, antlered Death.

I'm not insane. The truth is out there. More than a million motor vehicles per year hit deer in the United States; the number's climbing. Pennsylvania ranks fourth or fifth, depending on the study, in deer-related accidents per driver. Nationwide, car-deer crashes kill an average of two hundred people per year. September and October are the most perilous months, dusk and dawn the most dangerous hours. A Pennsylvania driver's approximate chance of hitting a deer during the course of a year is one in seventy.

And yet the highway beckons. The highway has sung to me since 1960, when Sandy and I drove from Cleveland to Los Angeles, mainly on the Mother Road: Route 66. No man is truly author of his fate, but Sandy tried, as all men must, and moved Lucille and three sons—I am the oldest—out west to find his fortune, which turned out to be a long war with severe bipolar disorder. Lucille and my wee brothers flew. I was eight and rode with him across America.

Never had I been so happy as a son, side by side with him, a thirty-three-year-old recently retired carpet-and-tile-store manager driving a 1954 Ford, with his eight-year-old son, a husky boy with a yellow T-shirt, powder-blue shorts hiked to the waist, and orthopedic shoes. In the few photos I have from the trip, I'm wearing his watch, its flexible band shoved up my chubby arm. We are men on the road, on our own, on the move, free of time and place.

That highway song, unlike the rest of me, has not grown old. Six hours until dawn, when those homicidal antlered pricks start foraging, and so I—exulting in wine-and-gold bliss, oozing manhood, and, not least, craving my wife and her vegan chili—ease into the Accord, cautious not to torque my manly back, and go.

An hour west of Cleveland, I pass the Lordstown plant, where the local UAW workers' uprising of 1972 failed to ignite the struggle that might've changed the fate of assembly-line workers crushed by automation and Japanese competition. After three weeks, national union leaders, fearing that other locals might rise up, connived with GM to sell them out. Back then, 7,000 Lordstown workers built the Chevy Vega, an especially ugly and unsafe car. These days, 4,500 produce

Cruzes, and half of the vast parking lot is now filled with solar panels, not cars.

Comes the long curve into PA, and the night grows darker as the woods grow thick. Past Oil City, Emlenton, and Knox—out there past the tree line, folks are home in bed, but onward rides this laptop warrior, on past Clarion, past Brookville and DuBois, and on to Clearfield, exit 120—just past I-80's high point east of the Mississippi, a towering 2,250 feet above sea level.

The night is velvet, endless. I swap Van Morrison for *London Calling* and reflect on the Lordstown wildcatters. Youngstown, Akron, Cleveland—proud cities, filled with household heroes, crawling to achieve self-creation before we vanish. We yearn to live right—we're not animals here, after all, whatever our excuses—but we are the very same creatures who ate from the Tree of Knowledge and needed a Maker to command us not only not to kill each other, but merely to honor our own parents.

Ach. Fate is not an open highway—it's Death's turnpike. It's Mile Run, with NO SERVICES plastered across the exit 199 sign. The road may stay time, but not the jug of coffee I grabbed at the Clearfield CoGo's. I carry a note in my wallet from a urologist, in case the law's long arm espies my short third leg, but I'd rather soil my drawers than urinate on the side of an interstate. Death or glory, my ass.

No services. The prostate swells. Soon or late, each man becomes Polonius, and trust me on this: your prostate is not your friend. We are finally ruled by powers beyond our power—by love, by death, by metaphysics and biochemistry. Our work is to manage our dread, to let our hearts go, to call forth whatever love we can muster. We work to earn more than a living wage. We work to earn our living. We work to make it to exit 224.

LeBron and Lee Jenkins said, "In Northeast Ohio, nothing is given. Everything is earned. You work for what you have." This is no less true in every corner of the world, but here it is the credo of the disrespected, a fundament of the religion of resentment. The worth, spiritual and economic, of even a sad-sack team to a Rust Belt riven by race and class and economic ruin, hope and jobs gone, abandoned and ignored, is beyond my power to calculate. A championship? Reveling in public glory? The feeling is beyond my power to imagine, even in the darkness of I-80.

If LeBron can win a crown for Cleveland, anything's possible. Even some of the pissant savants who think the league began play when they were boys might finally admit that Michael Jordan is the second-greatest player of all time.

Just to be clear, I lived in Iowa City from 1984 to 1991— seven years that felt like seventy—where SportsChannel Chicago was on the cable menu, so I watched nearly every Bulls game, suffered through Red Kerr and Jim Durham calling his dazzling youth with breathless lust. But this is not about that, or The Shot, his buzzer-beater that tore out the heart of one of the best pre-LeBron Cavs teams, in 1989.

Michael was otherworldly, but it does his greatness no

disservice to recall that he came into the NBA after three years' study under Dean Smith at UNC; that his Bulls teams got dropped in the first round of the playoffs in each of his first three seasons, and never got further until Scottie Pippen showed up. Even then—with two Hall of Fame–bound prodigies—the Bulls were curb-stomped for three years more by the Pistons in the Eastern Conference Finals. Then Detroit's Bad Boys fell into decrepitude, and Michael Jordan began harvesting rings in an NBA diluted by expansion, facing no true rival, and became, by unanimous consent, the GOAT.

Bosh. Believe it or not, there was an NBA before you were born, with players as great as Michael Jordan. I saw Oscar when his Cincinnati Royals played a slate of home games at the old Cleveland Arena, rubble now, on Euclid Avenue. I saw Chamberlain and Russell, and Elgin Baylor, an early version of early LeBron. I saw Kareem, the greatest big man, back when he was Lew Alcindor, battling old Wilt in the low post, in 1969.

It's hard to compare epochs with your eyes, and hard to normalize performance metrics across generations. But it is true beyond dispute that, in toto, the best athletes get better over time, in every sport. LeBron James is the finest basketball player ever. In *The Whore*, where I spit upon his heart, I said the same—because it was the truth, because that's why losing him hurt so much. His size, speed, and strength; his focus, vision, and intelligence; his tolerance for hard contact and his durability; his ability to attack or defend any opponent, to find every open teammate and get him the ball—he is the purest player ANY of you have ever seen.

I kiss the rings. No Cleveland fan disparages the rings. But don't count Michael's six and discount Bill Russell's eleven. And don't remind me that Michael's Bulls never lost an NBA Finals unless you recall he won ALL of them with Scottie beside him and Phil Jackson on the bench.

LeBron had no Pippen; he had Damon Jones and Donyell Marshall, Larry Hughes and Mo Williams, Sasha Pavlovic and Zydrunas Ilgauskas. He didn't play under Dean Smith and Phil Jackson; he came to the NBA from high school, and he was coached by Paul Silas and Mike Brown. The season after LeBron left, the Cavs won FORTY-TWO fewer games. When Michael left the Bulls, their win total dropped by two.

I saw Michael bend the NBA to his craft and his will, and I've watched LeBron do the same while not punching teammates, taking thirty shots a game, and hiding behind "Republicans buy shoes, too" every time he was asked a non-basketball question. If you care about the truth, study the metrics—win shares, VORP, whatever lights up your mom's basement—and you'll see them running neck and neck, Black Jesus and King James. And only one of them is still playing.

AT LAST EXIT 224, Danville. There's a Best Western, and, better, a men's room close to the front desk. Best of all, the Geisinger Medical Center is right there, in case of a nondeer emergency. Three or four hours of sleep, 126 miles more, and I'm home. I shall wake at dawn, roll over, and go back to sleep until the sun has fully risen and the deer are done with breakfast. If I time it right, I'll miss the hellish morning rush hour in East Stroudsburg, a mile before I-80 ducks south past the ridge of the Delaware Water Gap and exits Pennsylvania.

Thanks to good bad luck and Chekhov's sound advice, I run over the deer with my name on it just past Buckhorn, exit 232, not long after it already has been killed and somewhat flattened, a young buck in stately, plump repose sideways across the right lane. I don't see it until I'm too close to swerve, which is inadvisable in any case. The Accord jolts twice in quick succession as its tires hit the corpse, but holds steady.

MOTHERFUCK. I'm not dragging anything I can hear, feel, or smell, and I need an oil change anyway—I'll ask the dealership to power-wash the undercarriage while they're at it. I drive on. I can almost taste Lisa's vegan chili, thick with bulgur, aflame with spice. She waits in North Jersey, my Penelope, my Molly Bloom, my Ruth, my Julia Child. If I don't hit another deer, I can make it home before the kid gets out of school.

THE DAY OF ATONEMENT, the highest of the High Holy Days, a.k.a. the Days of Awe, a.k.a. the Ten Days of Repentance, from Rosh Hashanah to the Big Kip. The rules are simple: go to shul to pray, abstain from food and drink for twenty-four hours, sundown to sundown, and, uh, repent.

I am sitting in a Presbyterian church in Montclair, New Jersey. Our synagogue, Bnai Keshet, outgrew its chapel years ago for High Holiday services. On Yom Kippur, the day Elohim inscribes your name in the Book of Life—or doesn't inscribe it; Judaism gives no gimmes—even the least pious Jew makes a cameo, and sits next to my wife.

She's a Jew named Elizabeth Riley Brennan—a convert. Lisa was a self-exiled Catholic, and when we conceived a child, we went with Jew. It wasn't a religious or spiritual choice to me; it didn't feel like a choice at all. I'll grapple lifelong with my higher power, whom today I choose to call Lisa, but I'm no monotheism enthusiast. Yet I love Jews, love being a Jew, and there are few enough of us in the world that I wanted my son to know that he is the son of a member of the tribe.

The rabbi wears white, because purification. He is a splendid rabbi, a learned, gentle young Warriors fan from Northern California. The congregants, too, are exemplary: leftist Jews of various shades and gender blends and ages, so many faces aglow with kind spirit—I can't stand it. Maybe because the Jews who raised me once slapped the gum out of my mouth on Yom Kippur, when I was fresh from Los Angeles and unfamiliar with the drill, I don't fast. I do hold grudges.

I don't fear G-d any more than I fear Frankenstein's monster. I fear humans. It seems to have turned out that while I strongly support the concept of Jews, I don't actually feel comfortable around them, not in a synagogue, and surely not in a *goyische* pew.

On the bright side, a small "Prayer Request" card, pale yellow, sits in the bookrack, offering the chance to be included in the pastor's prayers for "thanksgiving and intercession."

"In our prayers today, please pray for:" it reads, and there's space to write below, so with the pencil stub in the bookrack, I fill it in:

Kyrie
Kevin
LeBron
Dion
Andy

"(continue over, if needed)," it suggests, but I don't want to be one of those greedy Jews. I stick the Big Three up top, with Kyrie and Kev first, because they're prone to injury; Dion Waiters, because he is another young lottery pick struggling to find his purpose in the league beyond bricking threes and bawling "AND ONE!" whenever he tries to finish at the rim; and Anderson Varejão, an elder now, always injured, who spent his early year with the Cavs flopping backward in the face of the enemy, hard, looking to draw charging fouls, and now whiles away his waning seasons cashing paychecks and sitting on the bench.

Andy deserves a prayer, too.

I knew it was a long shot. I'd already tried the same thing at the Wailing Wall, in 1968, imploring *Hashem* to crown the Browns and the Indians—the Cavs did not yet exist—in the customary fashion, writing my wish on a tiny scrap of paper and wedging it into a crack between the massive stone blocks of the last remnant of the Second Temple. I had weathered five years of Orthodox hell by then, living with Lucille and my brothers in her parents' one-house shtetl in Cleveland Heights, while in Los Angeles, Sandy wed his Catholic lover and had a Catholic son. By 1968, I was fifteen and feral—ask my poor brothers—and my mother's extended family paid to send me to *Eretz Yisrael* for three months, in the hope that Masada and falafel might tame me.

Hah. All I gave a damn about was Cleveland sports. I didn't go to *shul* or pray. I gave no thought to politics or gods. I wrote irate letters to sports columnists, phoned bilious Sweet Pete Franklin's radio show to spew on-air. I knew no higher power.

Fatherhood at forty-seven tamed me. Being the apostate son of an apostate son tamed me. Fear tamed me, too. Now here I am, sheltering in the house of the Hebrew Hammer, my *tallis* drooping between my legs—and here, my son, here is my gift, your legacy: a jealous, trigger-happy Lord, circumcision, Yom Kippur, and Cleveland sports.

The kid's my kind of Jew: fiery, doubting. For his Bar Mitzvah, he had to explicate a Torah portion about Korach, a post-Exodus Levite leader who, for questioning Moses's authority as Yahweh's sole capo, was swallowed by the earth along with his family, friends, and land, with a fireball thrown in for good measure, immolating 250 of Korach's community, just to quiet any blowback.

Judah went pro-Korach in his *d'var*, deeming him "a noble man with good intentions," calling out Moses for snitching, and adding, "That does not sound like any G-d I want to worship."

The congregation wasn't thrilled, but I chose not to take it personally; I know where he learned his shtick. After we came home from seeing *The Incredibles*, when he was five, he looked poker-faced at me and said flat out, "Why couldn't you have been a superhero instead of a fat know-nothing, which is what you are?"

Wowed by *know-nothing* and unsure if I should slap or throttle him, I shouted for Lisa to come in from the kitchen and repeated his slander to her.

"JUDAH!" she hollered.

"What?" He shrugged, eyes wide, palms up. "I LOVE him."

JUDAH'S HERE, LISA'S HERE, and I'm feeling fresh, a worthy Jew—just look at this young Jew I helped make; look at his mother, an enlistee. I'm wearing my skullcap, mouthing what I can recall of the prayers, standing when instructed, though I'm still stiff from driving, and my right hip—ah, never mind. No tallis; I wore one for the bar mitzvah, but I'm not a prayer-shawl guy. Still, I'm a Jew in his shul with his wife and son on Yom Kippur. So inscribe me for one more year at least, O Master of the Universe, with Whom I hedge my bets. *Sh'ma!*

Shit. I entirely forgot about the martyrology service, an

Ashkenazi prayer ritual begun centuries ago in remembrance of ten Talmudic sages slain by Hadrian after the Second Temple fell. What with history's surplus of butchered Jews, there are many other souls to mourn, and despite the cruel denial of my credentials, our martyr today is another writer, Danny Pearl, the *Wall Street Journal* reporter beheaded by Khalid Sheikh Mohammed in Karachi in 2002.

I did not know him, but at a Reconstructionist synagogue in Montclair, New Jersey, a half hour from Manhattan, someone surely did. There is a handout stuck in our prayer books, both sides single spaced, kicking off with a poem for the "haunted, harried, persecuted souls / who never had a choice / who've huddled all together in a corner / and press each other still and quake."

No matter that the poet Chaim Bialik was writing about a blood libel–based, priest-led, two-day pogrom in Kishinev, the capital of Bessarabia, that started after Easter Sunday services in 1903 and ended with 120 dead Jews. They're all martyrs: the slaughtered sages, the suicidal zealots on Masada, the Six Million, Danny Pearl.

I'd rather think about the Cavs, whose preseason begins tomorrow night, than dwell upon my tribe's insistence on its unique historical victimhood. I get it. Lucille's father himself lost five brothers and their wives and children at Auschwitz, and I have prayed at Sobibor, a factory of slaughter. I get it, but I don't like it, don't like the way the *Shoah* has turned Judaism into a cult of skeletons and pity. By the time I was born, in 1952—seven years after the camps were liberated—

two things, one of them true, had been made plain to every Hebrew American: Ashkenazi culture and history had been nearly erased, along with most of the world's living Jewry; and the Six Million were herded, meek as sheep, to the ovens.

It burned my father's ass that anyone thought of Jewish men as weak. Sandy came up hard on Kinsman Road, a ghetto of tradesmen, thugs, and Communists. His father was a two-bit Polish hood who left the house during the Great Depression and never came back. His mother, whose own depression lasted lifelong, gave Sandy, the youngest of five children, to her baby brother Julius Raab, né Rabinowitz, an MD with a side specialty performing abortions in the 1940s and '50s. Sandy liked to boast that both his fathers did time in federal prison, which they did. Willy Pelz went up the river to Lewisburg, exit 210A, for bootlegging; Doc Raab pled to tax evasion and did his stretch in Leavenworth.

Maybe Sandy overcompensated. He always owned a handgun and talked tough. He once told my brother Michael a story about punching a shipmate off the deck and into the drink for calling Sandy a kike. I never heard about that from him, but over the years I've met a lot of Jewish men my age who heard some version of that story from their fathers, uncles, or older cousins, set in the service or a steel mill or a tavern. Their tales, true or not, required no rabbinical interpretation.

Those soul-dead motherfuckers hate us.

Throw the first punch.

Martyr or be martyred.

Reconstructionist theology rejects the idea of the Jews as a Chosen People—too divisive. I can go either way, depending on the quality of the pastrami, but without illusion; now, as ever, the mass of humanity NEEDS us to blame.

"If you ever forget you're a Jew," wrote Malamud, "a gentile will remind you."

No need. I don't forget for a second that I live among human animals and their idiot gods. Let my son go forth open eyed into a world where people still worship the Jew as trickster, parasite, and scum, let him go in the spirit of *tikkun olam*, let him do his best to live right and heal humanity, armed always with a weapon or a plan.

THE SERVICE IS ENDLESS. My patience is not. I kiss my wife, nod at the kid, and leave. I pull this vanishing act every Yom Kippur. I get sweaty, hungry, angry, and I'm Judah's age again, fifteen, imprisoned in my family of birth. Let me go forth, sit on the steps outside, and settle down.

Yom Kippur. Pastrami. Danny Pearl. Chopped liver.

Atone. ATONE. *ATONE.*

That's when it hits me—sitting alone, apart from the congregation where I need no credentials to belong and to be loved, loathing my people as I loathe myself—that I owe LeBron James more than an overwritten apology, not for the sake of credentials, but for my soul. Judah has never read *The Whore of Akron.* As far as I know, he's never read anything I've written, and that's fine with me—there's stuff in there about me and Lisa we're all better off with him not knowing. I didn't think about that as I wrote an angry book. I did not think even once about hurting my own son. I'm a writer, damn it. The truth takes no prisoners. I speak my heart. All that crap. And now I realize that I also gave no thought to the insult and pain my words might inflict on LeBron's children someday.

My stomach churns. Enough fasting—it's already past noon. Inscribe me, don't inscribe me: I need chili. I am past atoning. I am not media, no longer even a fan. I'm a boil on the armpit of the finest athlete Northeast Ohio has ever grown.

Pariah. No man, Jew or gentile, is truly author of his fate, and so I shall roll with this.

Pariah.

7

HOMECOMING KING

The day before the Cavs open the regular season against the Knicks, I pick up Judah at school and we light out for Cleveland. It's Wednesday, so he's going to miss two days of school, which makes me happier than it does him. He has a computer science project due Monday, or we'd stay for the Browns game on Sunday, too. Led by a new head coach, they've started the season by winning four of their first seven games, including a beatdown of the Pittsburgh Steelers, rare as a comet. Cleveland has always been at heart a football town, and the Browns kidnapped to Baltimore by that decomposing rodent known in life as Art Modell were replaced by zombied clowns, but 4-3 is 4-3, and the town's on fire.

In fact, there should be time enough to catch the Brownies and still get to school on time Monday morning.

"No," Judah says.

It's a one p.m. kickoff. It's doable. In theory.

"We'll see," he says. "I'm already going to miss two days, and I have a lot of work."

I HASTEN TO EXPLAIN that I'm not the sort of father who'd encourage his kid to ditch even a single day of school for something trivial. This is The Return we're talking about. And as long as we're in town, why shouldn't he see his first Browns game? He'll ace his classes anyway. He always does. He gets that from the Brennan side—from mine, he can look ahead to back hair—plus he knows the secret:

He works his ass off.

I've always told him, all the talent in the world amounts to zilch without hard work. Trust the effort, I'd say, and the right results will come. Don't soil your nest, don't let the sun catch you crying, don't ever forget that fortune favors the bold. Once he realized that I was full of shit, that most men, unlike me, don a pair of pants and a shirt with buttons and go out to face the world every day, he understood.

IT WASN'T CHEAP TO find good seats. I paid too much, five grand for the pair. Even I know that this is insane, but it's a once-in-a-lifetime event, and it's me and Judah, and I am a big shot magazine guy with a side gig at ESPN. Could be just a smidge of bipolar in the mix, too. No clue how that happened. Sandy Raab.

The Cavs have come through their seven preseason games looking like a team and coach who've never worked together, which, of course, is precisely the case. David Blatt—who was hired to lead an inept, dispirited team, a team that, during their four preceding, post-LeBron, seasons, won 97 games and lost 215, rarely putting up a fight—now finds himself, having never coached a single minute in the NBA, even as an assistant, the nominal boss of LeBron, whose homecoming essay name-checked Irving, Waiters, and Tristan Thompson, referring to Blatt only as the "new coach."

"I get a thrill out of bringing a group together and helping them reach a place they didn't know they could go," LeBron added, gently placing the new coach's gonads in his pocket.

None of this has gone unnoticed. The local paper, which was once upon a time an actual newspaper known as the *Plain Dealer*, is now a clanking website called Cleveland.com, and has hired three full-time Cavs reporters to sniff for farts, and all the national media have deployed to report the Greatest Story Ever Told: LeBron's. LeBron helped the Cavs recruit the players he wants to play with, flew off to Brazil and China for Nike, shot *Trainwreck*, and with $53 million in annual endorsements, passed Tiger Woods to become pro sports' most precious individual brand.

Blatt? He's the Pharisee with the whiteboard, the rookie who cooled his heels for a month until LeBron found time to meet up, the Tel Aviv rebbe eager to teach an intricate Euro-Princeton offense—all five players running, cutting, and passing the ball—to the team's new self-proclaimed leader, the best player in the NBA.

I don't know the intricacies of the game, but I have been studying Blatt carefully, including his Princeton thesis, and I have uncovered two things: in his twenty-one years of coaching overseas, his teams have won seventeen championships;

and I enjoy saying his name over and over—David Blatt, David *Blatt*, DAVID *BLATT*—raising my voice until the dog jerks awake and looks at me in alarm.

The rest of the house is sleeping. I'm watching Blatt at a YouTubed press conference from May, after his Maccabi Tel Aviv team upset Real Madrid in overtime for the EuroLeague championship—a month before the Cavs hired him. That's when I uncover a third thing: Blatt's full of himself. Mighty full.

He begins by asking if any of the reporters are aware of Steve Jobs's last words.

"Did anyone see or hear what he said before he passed away?"

Silence. So Blatt explains that Jobs was a great leader and visionary, and asks again if any of them know his dying words, and shakes his head in wonderment at this gaping hole in the fabric of their knowledge of the great wide world.

"I can't believe you didn't see that story," he says.

He's smiling, very pleased—Maccabi was an underdog all the way to the title—and pleased to add his own wisdom to Jobs's.

"The last word he said was 'Wow,'" Blatt says, pausing to let the syllable echo. "Think about how wonderful that is, how positive that is, how optimistic that is—a man with his dying breath says 'Wow.' That means he saw something going forward that gave us all some hope."

Jobs's sister, delivering her eulogy, quoted the dying man as repeating "Oh, wow" three times, and it's possible that

Jobs wasn't feeling entirely positive at the moment; in any case, it's an odd way to begin a press conference. Blatt's point turns out to be optimism, the ingredient coaches need to "lead your men to bigger and better things, or lead them out of the dark when they don't see."

The seminar lasts almost four minutes.

"I'm really happy with the message we sent to coaches everywhere," he concludes. "You can do more with less, as long as you do it right."

Yeesh. I've seen this kind of thing before. Blatt's been the smartest guy in the room most of his life, but he needs to let you know that he is, and the only way he knows how is by letting you know that you're not. Seventeen titles in twenty-one years is nice, and he's doubtless the only NBA head coach who ever served in the Israeli Defense Forces—Blatt grew up twenty miles west of Boston, and is a dual citizen; his wife and children stayed in Israel—but the NBA isn't the Euro-League, where the head coach is king. Those seventeen chips don't shine here. And smart as Blatt might prove himself to be, he's not wise enough yet to know that he isn't smarter than LeBron.

THE DRIVING IS SWEET. I-80 winds into the setting sun, and we pull off in Clearfield, exit 120, two hundred miles from the Q. We slept at the Hampton Inn here in late January 2009, on a trip to Detroit in a 556-horsepower beast, a Cadillac CTS-V I was driving for an *Esquire* story about

General Motors. That was a great father-son trip. Judah saw his first jackknifed truck, in a snowstorm on I-90, and we sat in a GM conference room watching Barack Obama's first inauguration on TV, and he felt what one hundred per hour feels like. Best of all, no Cleveland team lost.

There are plenty more downscale lodging options in Clearfield, but Hampton's a solid choice for an elderly Jew, and Penn Highlands Hospital is only 3.8 miles away.

My hospital-proximity issues, by the way, began in 2008, the year before the Detroit trip, when I decided to goy up and take the lad fishing. We drove to Cooperstown, New York— his first trip to the Baseball Hall of Fame, his first chance to bask in the glow of the Tribe's rich history—and got on a boat, and caught a few fish, and at dinner shared a plate of brined shrimp and scallops, as outdoorsmen without regard for kashrut will, and shortly found out that he's allergic to shellfish.

Nothing in my literary training helped me recognize his swelling gums and itching throat as anything but metaphors— he'd had fried shrimp, clams, and oysters on Cape Cod years ago, with no symptoms—until he broke out in hives. By chance or grace, there's a great hospital in Cooperstown, the Bassett Medical Center, and we made it there in five minutes, and hung out until the Benadryl kicked in. Then went back to the motel and I watched him sleep all night.

No man is truly author of his fate, much less his son's, but you control what you can. Within us and without lurks death—better to stay near an ER if possible.

We saw the Hall of Fame the next morning, checked out Howe Caverns on the way back home, and ran over a vulture. I think it was a vulture. Big fucking bird. I slowed down, figuring it'd get out of our way, what with the wings and all, but all it did was duck.

We heard the thumps as we rolled over it, and I stopped a few yards down the road and saw the bird in my rearview mirror—still standing, looking back at me. Judah saw it, too. The kid and I looked at each other and drove away, and both of us were quiet for a long time after that.

"You think we should've gone back to see if it was okay?"

It looked okay. I'm not good with wildlife.

"To say the least."

That turned out to be a pretty good trip, too, though maybe not so much for the bird.

WHAT I HEAR OUT of Cleveland is that the power struggle between Blatt and LeBron commences before the team's first practice, when LeBron, with Blatt's permission, holds a players-only meeting. I don't doubt this for a second, nor do I care. I know something better: only one man alive craves a title more than me, and it isn't Blatt.

I saw what happened early in LeBron's first season in Miami, when the Heat were still learning to fit James, Wade, and Bosh, and losing as many games as they won. The young Heat head coach, Erik Spoelstra, called out LeBron in practice for goofing around, followed quickly by anonymous reports that some players felt that Spoelstra wasn't the right coach for the team. The hoo-ha lasted for a couple of weeks, until Pat Riley, team president and legendary martinet, let LeBron know that Spoelstra wasn't going anywhere.

That lesson in leverage wasn't lost on LeBron. He was committed to Miami for four years; the deal he signed with the Cavs to come back gives him the option to leave after this season. There are tens of millions of reasons for doing so—the salary cap will soar next year, inflating his maximum salary—and no one, me least of all, quite believes that he'll leave the Cavs again. Nobody quite believed he'd leave the first time, either. The fear is real. It's Cleveland, after all. And it's LeBron.

Yet it's not the same LeBron. He was twenty, in his second season with the Cavs, when Dan Gilbert bought the team and fired the head coach with eighteen games left in the season and the Cavs fighting for a playoff spot. He spent his next five seasons playing for Mike Brown, a good, good man and a bad head coach, and when Dan Gilbert fired Mike Brown and hired Byron Scott as LeBron weighed his free-agency choices, LeBron pledged his troth to Pat Riley, who held LeBron's first Heat preseason camp at an air force base, where the players were confined to quarters two hundred miles from Miami, to get their minds right. And with King James playing the best basketball of his life, the Heat reached the Finals in all four of his seasons in Miami, and won two crowns.

LeBron paid the physical price for those championships, and he's now thirty-one. Blatt's offense looks fine in the preseason—when the Cavs run it—but LeBron's jump shot is shaky, and Kyrie rolls an ankle and sits out three pre-season games, and the whatever-shall-we-do-with-Kevin-Love question—similar to the conundrum that arose with Chris Bosh in Miami that first season—starts asking itself after the very first preseason game, and it's plain to see that LeBron, not Blatt, is calling plays more often as he brings the ball upcourt.

This worries me. Great success doesn't *breed* arrogance—great success *requires* arrogance. This applies to both men, but only one doesn't yet know all that he doesn't know, and it isn't LeBron.

I'm pulling for my landsman Blatt, but I'm worried for him. Overseas, the season and the games are much shorter, there is far less travel and far more practice time, the rules of play and the officiating differ in ways large and small—and then there is the matter of culture, not just in terms of player-coach relationships, but also in the broader context of race in America.

Nobody talks openly about this, of course, but it is omni-present. The NBA is an African American league, and its styles of play, fashion, and language have all become medi-ums of African American artistry as rich and deep as jazz. No league matches the NBA in terms of hiring minorities or condemning racism, but the fact remains that all the own-ers save Michael Jordan are white billionaires, nearly half of them Jews, including Dan Gilbert. The league commissioner is Jewish, as was his predecessor, who held the job for thirty years. There were issues in the past with cornrows and rap music and the need for the hired hands to appeal to—or at least not scare—white, suburban season-ticket buyers presumed to fear all men of color until they prove threatless.

The NBA's image has softened and its revenues have soared since the olden days of AI and Artest and Latrell and Rasheed. The league's biggest stars are brands unto themselves, and in business with empires that move goods across the globe. It's easier to play nice, not make trouble, live the lesson Michael taught: Republicans buy shoes, too.

But something's changing. When former Clippers' owner Donald Sterling was caught on tape telling his girlfriend he didn't mind if she slept with black men as long as she didn't "bring them to my games," NBA players unified against his bigotry. His own team was prepared to boycott a playoff game, and wore their practice jerseys inside out, hiding the Clippers logo.

So did the Heat, in solidarity.

"There's no room for Donald Sterling in our league," LeBron said, the day after the news broke.

Our league. He isn't wrong. Adam Silver, the commissioner, understood. He fined Sterling $2 million, banned him from any role with the team he owned, and banished him from attending any NBA game. He vowed to force Sterling to sell the Clippers—which would require voting support from twenty-two of the NBA's twenty-nine other franchises. Hard to imagine the franchise dumb enough to defend Sterling's ownership on the basis of his private property rights—none did—and Donald Sterling, lawsuits blazing, peddled the Clippers to Microsoft CEO Steve Ballmer for $2 billion. Sterling paid $12 million for the franchise in 1981, which disqualifies him for any future martyrology.

The Jewish Question came up at Adam Silver's initial press conference, when a Jewish journalist named Howard Megdal began a question by noting that both the commish and Sterling, whose birth name was Tokowitz, are "self-identifying" Jews, and asked if Silver's personal response involved "a specific kind of pain" and "a certain responsibility within the Jewish community."

And Adam Silver, bless his soul, recoiled a bit, and began his answer with, "I think my response was as a human being."

I don't know Megdal, who seems like a fine young man and suffered much ignorant opprobrium for asking, but I know what he was talking about: *tikkun olam,* the special obligation of the Chosen People to heal the world; the kinship that many American Jews have historically felt for African Americans; and the Twitter-driven, what-will-the-goyim-think conflation of Sterling's Jewishness and racism.

I don't know Adam Silver, either, but he also seems like a fine young man. He and Megdal didn't raise the fact that Donald Sterling is one of fourteen Jewish owners in a league of thirty teams. There are reasons, cultural and historical, that help explain the relationship between Hebrew Americans and basketball, and between Jews and money, and between African Americans and basketball, and between African Americans and money, and between African Americans and Jews, but to discuss such things is so much less comfy than silence; it's so pretty to believe we've all outgrown that beastly tribalism, no matter what our own towns and schools and dinner tables tell us.

Anyhow, LeBron already has revealed what the goyim think: *our league.* It's not a racial gauntlet, not a taunt—its arrogance is righteousness, made powerful by knowing that he speaks for many. Adam Silver, human being, knows this, too. This is not the Lordstown Chevy plant. The players are the game.

LeBron didn't just come back to lead the Cavs. He helped lead the charge when the players' union fired the executive director who'd run the shop for almost twenty years, and replaced him with Michele Roberts, a fierce Washington, DC, litigator who grew up in the South Bronx projects.

"They've got their union back," Roberts said when she was hired in July, "and I'm going to make sure they are empowered to take their union exactly where they want their union to go."

How much Blatt knows or cares about any of this, I don't know. It all bodes ill to me. It always does. The summer of 2014 has been bloody in post-tribal America: Eric Garner choked to death on camera in July, Michael Brown shot dead in Ferguson in August. LeBron James, who has two young sons, is surely paying attention, while Blatt prepares to introduce his offense. He might be the secret love child of James Baldwin and John Wooden, and he'll have to be. He's walking into his first NBA locker room with nothing but his dick in his hand—a fifty-five-year-old guy suddenly living alone in a downtown Cleveland apartment after thirty years playing, coaching, and raising a family in Israel, now expected to boss a team led by the best player in the league, the smartest, the most powerful, an aging, driven basketball king who has brought along his old-head friends, who has *lived* this, from the projects to the penthouse, and who knows that Blatt has not.

THE CAVS WIN SEVEN preseason games while often resting LeBron, who looks haggard and bounceless when he's out on the court. In the second-to-last game, a tough win over the Bulls, one of the Cavs' few potential Eastern Conference rivals, Blatt plays the Big Three heavy minutes, including thirty-two for LeBron, the most he's played this preseason by far. After the game, LeBron tells reporters that he'll skip the last game before the regular-season opener.

This seems to come as news to David Blatt when he's asked about it.

"I want my guys coming in healthy and happy," Blatt says. "If LeBron needs to sit another game, he'll sit another game. That's the priority."

My guys makes me happy. Love them, David Blatt. Cherish them. Choose your battles carefully, and don't be a dick. I didn't pay five grand to watch you stride the sidelines in your non-Izzy suit.

But no one knows what goes on behind closed doors.

On the day of that last preseason game, Savannah Brinson James, LeBron's wife, delivers a daughter. No wonder LeBron looks tired.

It crosses my mind to send a gift, a Tiffany silver spoon—a friend at *Esquire* gave us one when Judah was born, and it made us laugh and it made me feel like a million bucks. Maybe I am insane. It doesn't feel like a creepy or desperate thought in the moment. I've tried during the preseason to find a way past *The Whore of Akron*. My boss at *Esquire*, David Granger, reaches out to the PR guru who packaged The Return and is told *Never*. I follow that up with a short e-mail— "Though I may never get a chance to make personal amends, this will be a very different book" is my close—but I get no reply. I ask Tad Carper if he can send a message on my behalf to LeBron or his people: No. I meet Blatt's agent in New York City for lunch: *bupkis*. My agent tries to arrange a meeting with LeBron's agent—Rich Paul, the guy who blocked me on Twitter—and he fails, too.

How do you solve a problem like pariah? Atonement, credentials, a face-to-face apology: I'm not picky. My last hope is ESPN Films, a 30 for 30 documentary about Cleveland sports fans and their unrequited love. I'm an unpaid consultant—a few meetings, a few hours of filming me in Cleveland, at the grave of Ray Chapman, a stellar young Tribe shortstop a century ago, the one and only player in major-league baseball ever killed by a pitched ball, in 1920.

Then the documentary stalled for more than a year, and I figured it was dead, and finally the sports world would have incontrovertible proof: if the ESPN Films can't manage to produce a 30 for 30 about Cleveland sports misery, there *must* be a curse. But it has been resurrected, as *Believeland*, and the new director, Andy Billman, calls and asks for help.

Sure thing, so long as I don't have to weep again at Chappie's grave. We agree to meet in a coffee shop downtown, four hours before the first game of the season. Andy will bring his film crew, I'll bring Judah, and in June LeBron will lead the Cavs to the title, with the last scene featuring LeBron and me hugging it out while Judah cradles the Larry O'Brien trophy—named for the league's last heathen commissioner, who left office thirty years ago—glowing with a modicum of pride.

IT IS A BANNER day in Cleveland. It is a Nike banner, naturally, ten stories tall, 210 feet across, an exceedingly subtle black-and-white piece depicting LeBron in uniform from behind, arms extended like Christ on the Cross. In place of his surname across the back of his jersey, it simply reads CLEVELAND. There's a tiny puff of chalk dust floating in the light above his head, as if a small galaxy of his emanations of consciousness was heaven bound. Oh, and way up in the corner is the Swoosh of Nike, god of sneakers.

Fifteen workmen are three hours into the job of unfurling it when we get downtown at eleven a.m. for a hit with a *New York Times* film crew producing a documentary about the relationship of sports teams to the city. That's what media titans call it, a "hit." I assume that you're exactly as impressed as my son was. What's more important is that I am too ignorant to speak on the subject beyond hard-times lefty platitudes. I'm the guy who split in 1984, who pops in and out as he pleases, who still suckles at the teat of Cleveland sports for fun and profit.

There's only so long that you can watch a slow unfurling, so I ask the kid if he wants to try his first pastrami Reuben. I try to act casual about it. His relationship with foods other than shellfish is as calm and constructive as his mother's. Lisa's daily fare consists solely of Greek yogurt, vegetables, fruit, muesli, and a small portion of our dinner entrée—chili, or a roasted chicken, or mapo tofu—atop her bowl of spinach. The same bowl and chopsticks each night. Lisa will drink only coffee, tea, or water, and runs a hard five miles every day.

Because she would no sooner feed her newborn son formula than furniture polish, she breast-fed Judah throughout his first four years. I always say a silent thanks in front of Cal Ripken's plaque at the Hall of Fame, in Lisa's honor. Judah eats more, and likes it more, but he stops when he's full, and he won't eat fast food unless he's on the road with me. I don't want him ever to tremble with need at the thought of a pastrami Reuben. I don't want him worshipping *any* sandwich. But I do want him to meet the king of sandwiches, and I want him to see Slyman's.

There's nothing fancy or Jewish about Slyman's. It's a working-class breakfast and lunch spot, a small corner shop that closes when the corned beef runs out. It's five minutes east of downtown, on Saint Clair Avenue, and we're hitting it at the lunch rush, and there's a to-go line out the door, and everyone's talking about the Cavs, and our Reubens are fat and warm and salty in our mouths, and our cans of Coke are cold and sweet.

You should at least try the potato salad.

"I'm good."

It's very good after the pastrami. Cuts the salt.

"I'm full."

The crucial thing isn't the potato salad. The crucial thing isn't even the pastrami, because the Slyman's corned beef Reuben is no less wondrous in its way than its cousin, only softer and less salty. No, the crucial thing, the thing you must hold fast to from this day forward, is the irreducible truth of the Reuben: either it is a closed-face sandwich or it is not a Reuben.

"Got it."

I'm serious.

"I know."

Look, this isn't like the cinnamon-raisin bagel, which is a joke and a disgrace—BUT AT LEAST IT'S A FUCKING BAGEL! A sandwich with an open face is, by FUCKING definition, NOT a sandwich. And an open-faced Reuben is an abomination. Never forget. NEVER forget.

"I won't. I won't forget."

I'M NOT INSANE, JUST a little wound up. I have another hit at the public-radio station near my alma mater, Cleveland State, ranked 649th of 660 US colleges by *Forbes*. Lisa and I have endowed a small scholarship in the creative writing program there, and I've assured Judah that if Princeton doesn't come through, I can likely swing legacy admissions for him and Pip, our dog. We hustle back downtown to watch the rest of the banner drop. By the time we meet the film crew, at the Huron Square Deli, which is neither Slyman's nor a deli, I'm whored out. I just want to go to the game with my kid.

But I'm a trouper, damn it, and there's a sandwich. It's not a pastrami Reuben, but its face is closed and it is grilled and it tastes fine, if you respect bologna, which I do. ESPN films us—well, me—talking the same shit, about LeBron and Cleveland sports, the same shit Judah has heard me talk all day and all his life, but now we're at a lunch counter in Cleveland. Then they film us walking side by side down to the Q, into the setting sun.

The streets are alive, but it feels nothing like a playoff game—or a home opener, for that matter. I find my old spot on the bench near the Q's media entrance, to collect my emotions in tranquility, while Judah ambles off to shoot hoops at the Fan Fest plaza. From somewhere behind me, I can hear Kendrick Lamar onstage. Beyoncé and her hubby are here. Justin Bieber. Even the douchebag Geraldo. They've all come to Cleveland for Opening Night.

Me, I'm thinking of Jim Brown, who walked away from the Browns and quit pro football in 1965 after his ninth season, when Art Modell—whose spoor, even now, fouls the cosmos—tried to fine him for every day Brown missed summer training camp. Brown wasn't holding out for a better deal—he was pulling down a lordly sixty grand per season—he was in England filming *The Dirty Dozen*, trying to get a second career going as an actor. The production ran late, Modell starting huffing and puffing in the media, and Jim Brown, in reply, called it quits.

I loved Jim Brown. Early in 1964, before the Browns' last championship, he published a book I devoured, *Off My Chest*. In it, he wrote that his fans admired him "as they would a large piece of sculptured stone or a strong draft horse," just a "big brute." He spent fourteen pages on race relations, beginning with, "Among American Negroes in pro football today, there is one cardinal rule that each of us expects the other to follow: 'Assert your dignity,'" and ending with, "You have to wonder if the white man will ever begin to understand you."

In 1964, as one of the most visible and acclaimed athletes in the land, this took the balls of Jove. Black Muslims, Martin Luther King, the lack of commercial endorsements for athletes of color—*Off My Chest* wasn't what most white fans wanted to read. But Jim Brown's only brand was his truth. In 1966, after quitting the Browns, he came back to town and cofounded the Negro Industrial Economic Union, organizing black athletes, entertainers, and entrepreneurs in a self-help effort to build businesses in poor communities.

In 1967, JB's stature drew Muhammad Ali to Cleveland five weeks after Ali refused his army induction, to meet with

Brown, Bill Russell, the UCLA sophomore Lew Alcindor, and a roomful of black athletes and community leaders, in what has become known, to the extent that it is known at all, as the Ali Summit. The Greatest, all of twenty-five years old, his career and freedom at stake, explained his religious objections to serving and asked the group for its support. At a news conference, Ali got that support. Two weeks later, he was fined, stripped of his title, and sentenced to three years in prison for draft evasion.

Just south of the Q, outside the stadium where the Indians play, there are statues of Bob Feller and Jim Thome, but not of Larry Doby, who broke the American League's color barrier eleven weeks after Jackie Robinson played his first game for the Brooklyn Dodgers. Five blocks away, in Public Square, there's a statue of the city's founder, General Moses Cleaveland, a Connecticut lawyer who landed at the Cuyahoga's mouth in 1796, paid off the local natives, wished the surveyors luck, and left. He took the first *A* in his last name with him, never to return. But even in Berea—the West Side suburb where the neo-Browns' offices sit on a street named for Lou Groza, a tackle and kicker who played with Jim Brown, with a statue out front of Al Lerner, who helped Art Modell steal the real Browns and, mutatis mutandis, then bought the feckless new franchise from the NFL—there is no statue of Jim Brown.

THE Q HAS CHANGED since the Wine & Gold Scrimmage. There's a titanic HD video board hanging from the ceiling that would shame Jerry Jones. Dan Gilbert, with his customary refinement, has named it the Humongotron, and every square inch of it that isn't screen is—like every other horizontal surface inside the arena—plastered with ads.

Upon each seat rests a foil packet marked COMMEMORATIVE MOMENT, with the date, LeBron's own Nike logo, and instructions to each event attendee for its use. This is our "LeBron James pregame 'chalk-toss' bag," and our job is to "grab a healthy hand full & wait to join LBJ chalk toss."

Judah opens his bag. Confetti. White. Like chalk dust.

Don't do it, son. Don't let them own you.

Then the lights go down, and we doff our caps and cross our hearts for the anthem, but it isn't time yet. It is time for Nike. It is time to gaze upward at Humongotron to view "Together," the *Citizen Kane* of sneaker ads, the product of years spent studying the oeuvres of Lang, Riefenstahl, and Eisenstein, a slick two-minute black-and-white dream of the dream my hometown has been dreaming for fifty years.

The ad opens here at the Q, tonight, with LeBron's introduction. Already I am vertiginous. The sound picks up with the Cavs' PA announcer—compared with Crump, a Pavarotti—booming from the darkness. "From St. Vincent–St. Mary High School in Akron, Ohio . . ." and now we see LeBron as he jogs into the light of center court to huddle up his team.

"Bring it on in," LeBron tells them, and they gather tight. I see Kyrie. I see Andy. The angle is low now: we are in the huddle, too, rapt, as our king urges us to battle.

"It's time now," he says, shouting over the crowd roaring in the ad as we stand gaping in mute awe. "This is our city. We gotta do it for *them*, dawg. We gotta do it for *Cleveland*— they're waitin' on us. What we do tonight is gonna define what we're about."

As his voice trails off into the cheers, a quick-cut montage begins with shots of fans—swarming the court to join the team, swarming the streets and alleys, black and white, young and old, cops and winos, huddling like the Cavs, arms around each other's shoulders—one team, one town, united.

"Every single night, every single practice, every single game, we gotta give it all we got," LeBron says in the voice-over. "'Cause they gonna ride with us. Everything we do on this floor is because of this city. We owe them."

I may be getting an erection. I know I'm leaking from the eyes, sobbing so hard that Judah puts his hand on my shoulder to comfort me.

"'Hard work' on three, 'together' on six," LeBron tells his team as they prepare to break the huddle, and counts it down. His men all shout "HARD WORK!" on three and "TOGETHER!" on six, but LeBron's count doesn't stop, echoing as we cut again to five hundred extras thrusting fists and fingers to the sky, and through the eye of God I see the city's neoclassical bridges and boulevards, relics of the days when Lower Euclid Avenue was Millionaire's Row and Rockefellers and Carnegies lived here, framed in fresh glory as the Cavs and their fans holler—"One, two, three, *HARD*

WORK! FOUR, FIVE, SIX! *TOGETHER!"*—and all around the Q, fans staring up at the extras playing the fans on the Humongotron are punching the sky and hollering along.

The last shot, with music under, is the Cleveland skyline in mid-distance, set against a sky whose broken clouds provide the perfect background for "JUST DO IT" to dissolve into the Swoosh of God, in the center of the frame, just south of the Terminal Tower. Low and to the left, I spot the LeBron banner hung earlier today. Magic.

I just look at Judah. I can't speak. My throat hurts. My face is wet. My pants, thank God, are dry and untented.

"You okay, bub?" he asks.

I nod. I'm spent.

Usher finally croons the anthem and the actual players are actually introduced, LeBron tosses the chalk and everyone tosses the confetti. Judah, too. Not me. I didn't pay five grand to confirm my stupidity. I paid to see a win.

THEY LOSE, OF COURSE. LeBron looks exhausted from the start. At the half, the Cavs are up 44-42, but LeBron has already missed eight of nine shots, with four turnovers. The Knicks, a lousy team coming off a 24-point loss in their own season opener the previous night, dice the Cavs' defense in the second half and win 95-90.

Nobody's surprised. When the Cavs go down by nine midway through the fourth quarter, we're all moaning and groaning, but no one boos. Fifty years into a losing streak, why bother? It's not even a playoff game, and—HEY! There's *Johnny Football*!

Five fucking grand for ninety points against the fucking Knicks. So much for LeBronnukah.

You'll like Montclair State, son. We won't even have to rent out your bedroom.

No smile, much less a chuckle. Kid's pissed. Cleveland: of course they shit the bed. And as bad as the D looks, the offense is worse—half-Blatt, half-cocked.

"Better communication between me and Coach Blatt," Kyrie says after the game, "that's basically what it boils down to. I'm his point guard out there, and some things that I see—he has plays in his mind and I have plays in my mind as well. It's about what's going on out there, what he sees and what I see, and hopefully we can get on the same page pretty soon."

Yeah. *Hopefully*. Meanwhile, you're basically telling the media that you feel free to ignore the plays your rookie coach is calling.

The rookie coach can't afford to be so blunt.

"We're good when we move the ball," Blatt says. "And when we play without motion and without ball energy, that's what it looks like. And that is exactly what happened."

Okay. Not a big deal. It's exactly the kind of teaching moment that should be expected with a new coach and a gifted young guard whose first three pro seasons have been spent *not* passing the ball to inferior teammates. What truly worries me is LeBron, who ends up making only five of fifteen shots, turns the ball over eight times, and looks a little like a guy who might once have been LeBron James.

"It was a special night," James says. "It was exciting for the fans, exciting for the city, but I'm glad it's over. I didn't press. I was trying to focus as much as I could—I was throwing passes where I thought my teammates were. Those things will come."

The turnovers and bad shooting don't bother me nearly as much as Blatt leaving LeBron out there for forty-three minutes. That's a bad sign—worse than the loss. He looks tired and plays poorly from the tip to the buzzer, and yet Blatt keeps him out on the floor for all but five minutes, this despite the fact that the Cavs outscore the Knicks with LeBron on the bench.

Maybe Blatt's trying to focus, too. Maybe he's missing his family back in Israel. Maybe he's spreading his plumage by the only means any NBA head coach has—playing time. Whatever his reasons, leaving LeBron out there also stiffs LeBron's old-head crew.

James Jones never sees the court. Mike Miller plays three minutes. Shawn Marion plays only ten, and wonders why, aloud:

"We're all here to sacrifice something, but I'm here to help as much as I can, and do what I can, and if there's opportunities there, there's opportunities there. Tonight it just didn't come to me, and I got to understand that."

Oy. The Matrix isn't the player he used to be—he's in the sixteenth NBA season—but he's a no-doubt Hall of Famer, a guy who averaged thirty-two minutes per game as a starter on a good Mavericks team last season.

"It wasn't by design," Blatt explains. "It was the flow of the game. That's on me. Those guys need to play more."

Good news this is not. Opening night, and already they're all kvetching.

"It's one game," Dion Waiters reminds everyone. "We know people are going to make it seem like it's the end of the world. We got eighty-one more games, man."

I'm not reassured, man. This will be Dion's third season; the Cavs drafted him fourth overall, in 2012, after two years at Syracuse, coming off the bench, and four years at four different high schools around Philly. If Dion were only half as good as he thinks—I shit you not, he asked his college teammates to call him "Kobe Wade"—he'd be twice the player he is. For two seasons, I've seen Dion and Kyrie play like rivals, not teammates; Kyrie has learned that passing the ball to Dion means the ball's not coming back, and it isn't likely going through the hoop, either.

Frankly, I put Dion on the prayer card simply because he has moxie. And because LeBron and Lee Jenkins hoped LeBron would "elevate" Dion's game. Don't get me wrong: I don't regret putting Dion's name on the card. I just wish I'd have put Blatt on there, too.

8

SURVIVOR'S REMORSE

The Cavs have a plane to catch, for a game tomorrow night in Chicago. Judah and I head back to the condo. It's a quiet ride, ten, fifteen minutes on I-71. No deer. No montage. We're listening to the postgame interviews on the radio, listening and stewing, grunting and snorting with approval or disdain.

The condo is a three-bedroom unit in a faceless 1970s development called the Liberty Bell, a maze of beige and brown boxes so alike that I miss the turn into our cluster twice. I've got the third bedroom, but no one's ever here but me, so I sleep around. The only human I've met is the woman across the way, who kindly delivered a bowl of terrible chili when I was here for the Wine & Gold Scrimmage. She and her husband are trying to sell their unit; they have two sons, and had hoped to buy a house when the second boy arrived, but they're way underwater on the Liberty Bell note, and they're stuck.

I've read about such Clevelanders. I've seen them on *60 Minutes*. I was a version of their kids, the helpless offspring of the feckless. The difference is, I knew it. We were foundlings, three little boys from what they used to call a broken home. Everyone took pity on us. I wanted to kill them. It shamed me. It still shames me.

The town where I live now, Glen Ridge, is a New York City bedroom suburb too well groomed for light poles, which are hidden in backyards. On our streets, we have gas lamps, whose gentle glow makes it hell for the pizza guy to read an address. I was a pizza guy. Now I'm the guy calling Vinny's to find out where the fucking pizza is, the fat jagoff paying two small brown women to scrub his toilets twice a month.

Two toilets. This is the only house I've ever owned, the only home I've ever called my own, and the only place I've ever lived with two toilets. And I don't wish to clean them, nor do my wife and son. But I wish I could defecate in them free of shame, as Judah does.

He was born with two toilets, born to gas lamps, born to two aging drunks in recovery with enough money to stay in good hotels. And when he saw his first Hampton Inn, in Clearfield on the way to Detroit, he opened the door with his key card, paused, and took it in.

"Is this *it*?" he asked.

The condo has two toilets. But there's no TV and not much furniture. The only food we have is jerky, pretzel rods, and Bertman's Ballpark Mustard, the same sharp brown I squeezed on my Municipal Stadium hot dogs fifty years ago.

We break all of it out and eat off paper towels.

Just like camping, am I right?

Judah laughs. He began going away to camp for two weeks every summer when he was nine, after a classmate came back and talked about how cool it was. The first time we drove him there, a hundred miles away, I advised him that it takes courage for a fellow to change his mind, especially at the last minute.

"I haven't changed my mind."

We're getting close. You sure?

"I'm sure."

He loved camp. I was in awe of him, in awe of my wife, really. Her deal with him was simple: give him everything he needs in terms of touch and smell and taste and Mama's warmth. Forget the breast-feeding studies—newborn animals don't need studies. All they need is love, which if you're fresh from the womb means that breast, plus the woman attached to it.

I'm not saying there isn't room for debate about ancillary issues—minor from the newborn's point of view—or that I don't sound like a chauvinist asshole. There was no debate. Lisa kept him on the teat for as long as he craved her nourishment and comfort, and he kept milking her beyond his fourth birthday. After our first pediatrician gave us a case of soy formula and said Judah wasn't gaining enough weight, Lisa found another pediatrician the next day.

"She's *still* breast-feeding?" my mother would ask. "Is she going to breast-feed him at his high school graduation, too?"

One couples counselor counseled us to put Judah out of our bed and into a crib, for the kid's sake.

"He needs to learn to self-soothe," the counselor said.

I asked him if *he* slept alone every night.

"Why?"

Because every time I leave the house, I lose count of all the self-soothing people who were forced to self-soothe from birth on, and they mostly seem unsoothed to me. They seem downright pissed off. Including me. And Lisa.

They were Lisa's breasts, of course. I sacrificed and suffered nothing. She did. She left her journalism job, stuck him on the nipple, put him in a Bjorn, and walked him to the park every day year-round, and took him to Vermont and Maine for a week every summer to see her brothers and their families, and they'd all bike and hike and swim and sail while I stayed home with Pip, writing.

My deal with Judah was more complicated. I'm still not sure I understand it. I had no father after age ten, but I can still remember what he smelled like when I was small, and how large he loomed, and I assume that even a son born to a paraplegic dwarf thinks of his sire as the ruler of the world, a giant among men. So I didn't worry about my authority or his respect. I gave him all the authority and respect I could as soon as I could. I held him close, told him I loved him, told him I could never repay the clarity and joy he gave me, but I turned forty-seven soon after he was born, and I took seriously the actuarial truth beneath the mundane miracle of fatherhood: I'll be three score years and eight when he turns twenty-one.

I had his business cards and letterhead printed when he

was six. I could tell by then he was already smarter than me, although I still knew more than he did. He wasn't, thank God, any prodigy. He was just paying close attention. I taught him the double take, and how to play cards, and I showed him the family twelve-gauge, up on a shelf in my attic office he can't reach. I shared all the sad tools of my manhood save one, and he came equipped with one of those.

You can be anything you want to be, I told him then—except one thing.

"What?"

An editor.

"Why?"

Ask me when you're older. And don't become a writer if you can help it.

"I won't."

I also told him what I always wanted to hear, and never did: I had his back. Mama had the milk, I had the muscle and money, and I wasn't going anywhere. Every time he lost a tooth, the fairy left him a C-note. When he came home crying one day because some asshole was picking on him, I got in touch with the principal, but before I did, I went over to the bully's house for a chat. When Judah struck out to end a playoff game and cried, I cried, too.

From his birth, I tried to honor the basic truth: there now were two different men living under our roof, one grown, one fresh. *Three* men—because whenever something complex came up, in my working life or our marriage, I asked myself a question—What would Sandy do?—then I did the other thing. Granting that everyone, including Sandy, does the best he can, it wasn't hard to do better.

I DON'T KNOW WHY "Together" made me cry so hard. I understand why Cleveland and those teams mean so much to me; that became the main question as *The Whore of Akron* turned into a mission filled with hatred for an athlete whose fate had no real impact on my own. Cleveland and those teams gave me strength, a sense of permanence, pride, and self when I was down and out after Sanford and Lucille called it quits. I was angry, hurt, and trapped. I missed my daddy, two thousand miles away. Our sainted mother didn't just bad-mouth him every day; she was the kind of woman who also told me that I was just like him, and the special sort of monster who refused to let Sandy see our baby brother, Bob, on his yearly visits.

When my grandparents fought, sometimes they got physical, and if Lucille was at work—her brother the pharmacist got her a job as a dermatologist's secretary—brother Dave or I would have to call the cops. Bobby—my parents let me pick his name, hoping to avoid the enmity I showed to David when he followed me by two years, so he was Robert, my homage to the Indians' Hall of Fame pitcher Bob "Rapid Robert" Feller—had night terrors. David, who was also forced to suffer my bullying, would get sick before school.

I became a writer, and my life turned out great. Except for Cleveland sports.

It dawns on me, camping out in the saddest condo complex this side of Aleppo, sitting on a green plastic lawn chair at a barren kitchen table with my laptop—the kid's asleep upstairs—that part of what I'm feeling must be survivor's remorse, which also happens to be the title of a Starz series, executive-produced by none other than LeBron James, about a wealthy young baller from the hood.

I am not a wealthy young baller from the hood. LeBron grew up in exponentially tougher circumstances, starting with the facts of life and race in America, and he has stayed close to family and friends. I stay away. My model for survivor's remorse is Ipish, my grandfather, the man of my grandparents' house when my mother moved us back to Cleveland. He wasn't much older than I am today—these people had no birth certificates, and refused until their dying day to answer questions about their lives—and he came to America in 1905 or so.

Ipish—Yiddish for *stench*—wanted to become a painter and a writer and a cantor, and, failing at them all, spent his working life cleaning railroad cars at the New York Central yard downtown. Never drove. Spoke and wrote Yiddish. A greenhorn Jew who left his family in some village east of Bratislava and came to America to make bad. By the time I landed under his roof, he was frankly demented. He had built a sort of cage for himself in the unfinished basement—two-by-fours nailed together on three sides, no door—an imprisonment from which he freed himself only to eat or shit or fight or walk to shul.

The only explanation I ever heard for his behavior was that his whole family had stayed in Europe and died at Auschwitz. I have a letter sent to him from the Zionist Organization of America, dated September 26, 1944—its response to his inquiry six days before. He was trying to arrange for visas to Palestine via Turkey for his five brothers and their wives and children, along with sundry other kin, but he hadn't provided names and ages, and it would not have mattered anyway: months before, they'd all been herded into the Kosice ghetto in Slovakia and, along with 15,700 other Jews, sent to Auschwitz between May 19 and June 4, 1944, where—whether or not the ZOA knew it—they were liquidated.

"As for the people in Poland," the letter reads; maybe these were his cousins—"there is nothing we can do at the present time."

Tough loss, old-timer. I wouldn't want to watch your Starz series, and your contempt for my paltry suffering, like your furious insanity, now makes better sense.

I forgive you, you stanky prick. I even gave Judah your Hebrew name, Avram.

And heck, aren't we *all* somehow survivors? #toosoon. #itwillalwaysbetoosoon. #NO. Not like my grandfather, much less the parents of my friends who came out of the camps alive. My suffering and remorse were but a mayfly's by comparison with theirs. And like LeBron, I had a special gift. Not as special as LeBron's, but I knew by the time I turned eleven that I would be a writer, and I knew that I'd never settle for anything else.

The knowing—that was the gift. I was already writing, and even after I started getting paid for it once in a while, by which time I was already past thirty, I always figured to take my talents back to Cleveland one day and share them with my hometown. I'd be a *Plain Dealer* sports columnist, heir to the throne of Hal Lebovitz, the king of local columnists. I'd be the voice of the fan and write my literary fiction on the side. And I would have a seat at every home game for every team in town. Living the Dream.

Hal Lebovitz and I exchanged a few letters in the mid-1980s, when I was in Iowa City with my MFA and my then wife, who was a med student. I was writing short stories and I had a weekly general-opinion column for the *Daily Iowan* for a hundred bucks a month. I sent him some of my columns—he was the editor of the *PD* sports section by then—and he was less than encouraging, and found fault with my taste, for which I couldn't blame him, and addressed me as Steve, which pissed me off.

Just as well: By the time I left Iowa, in 1991, I'd already overshot the mark. By '93, I had a contract at *GQ*, working with David Granger and his crew. And it has been pure gravy ever since. I have the sweetest job in journalism, and I've had it for more than twenty years. I just paid five grand for two seats to a Cavs game, and took my son. Lisa and I have been together since '93, and our amour is still fou and our house is almost paid off. My cholesterol, thanks to her vegan chili, is 147, and while she can't hang the wash to dry on my erection, she never could.

Hal's long gone, *alev ha-shalom*, as is the Cleveland I knew, and I have thrived. Does it matter that Cavs lost? If Judah's a true fan, a letdown like tonight's game is a rite of passage, a taste of what the old man has lived his whole grown life. It's a good thing. And just like Dion said, it's one of eighty-two games before the playoffs even get going, and more of a celebrity circus than a sporting event.

What the hell is it I'm crying about?

I just want to see a championship with my son. That's it. That's all.

WE'RE UP AT THE CRACK of ten for breakfast at Bob Evans. The kid has never tasted biscuits and gravy. Hell, Judah's never even been inside a Bob Evans, an Ohio-based chain founded seventy years ago by none other than Bob Evans, a sausage-making genius from southern Ohio. It's our first trip to Cleveland without Lisa; foodwise, he has a lot of catching up to do.

Our waitress is Dolores, who could be in her forties, fifties, or sixties: I can't tell. There are places in Cuyahoga County where I can tell—Beachwood, Solon, Chagrin Falls—miles east of Cleveland proper, refuges to which my kind have fled. All I know about Dolores is that she looks tired.

I ask her how she's feeling. She's exhausted. Her shift here begins at seven, and when she's done, at two, she goes to work at a pharmacy chain down the road. Six days a week—sixty hours on her feet. Two part-time jobs. No benefits.

I tell Dolores this morning is the kid's first taste of sausage gravy.

"You want me to put a candle in it?" she asks him, and they both laugh.

The point, I tell Judah after she takes our order, isn't to feel bad for Dolores. That's way too easy. The point is to ask folks how they're doing, and to listen. They want to talk, *need* to talk. But you need at least as much to listen, to learn—even if all you learn is how good you truly have it. And you must tip well. Thirty percent. Cash, so they don't have to report it. More than once, I've left a twenty on the table in this town and had the waitress follow me to the register, thinking I'd left it by mistake. At Swensons' original location in Akron, doing deep reporting for *The Whore*—LeBron teethed on Swensons' Galley Boys—I gave a twenty to the carhop when he took away the tray and he had tears in his eyes when he realized I was serious.

We're splitting the order, because it's soccer season and the kid takes nutrition and fitness seriously, too. He likes the gravy, pronounces it outstanding—he loved the Reuben yesterday, and scarfed it all, no small task—but he leaves most of the bowl to me. I texted Lisa a photo of the Reuben. I don't wish to test her with the gravy.

Instead of staying over for the Browns game—one loss per Cleveland trip is plenty—we visit the Western Reserve Historical Society's special museum exhibit, *1964: When Browns Town Was Title Town*, part of the educational portion of our trip, which includes a drive-by of my grandparents' house at 1896 Staunton Road, up the hill, in Cleveland Heights.

There were rats living underneath the house. Huge rats. And even larger, two-legged rats upstairs.

"I know it was hard," he says.

It was hard, yeah. But nobody starved me. Nobody molested me. Nobody killed me. People do that to their children every day. In the long run, it was good for me. I knew that I had to carve out a life for myself. Everyone does, bub. The sooner you know it, the better.

I'm not telling him anything he hasn't heard or anything he wasn't born already knowing. He started moving away the day he began crawling; nobody had to teach him. He'll be moving on soon enough. He's not me, not the one who fears that every separation is an abandonment; I am. And it's not his pity or respect I crave—I just need to talk, and he needs to listen and to learn, even if all he learns is how lucky the two of us have it.

THE CAVS ARE MAGIC that night, or maybe the night is magic. It's Halloween, and the Cavs beat the Bulls, in overtime. Down five with under a minute left, they roar back to tie the game, and with LeBron scoring a quick eight points in OT and Kyrie icing two free throws to finish off the win, they're 1-1. Huzzah.

LeBron's final line is thirty-six points on thirty shots— four fewer than Kyrie and Love combined—in forty-two minutes on the second night of a back-to-back. God damn it, Blatt. I get it: the Bulls and Cavs are conference, division, and historical rivals—I'm pleased when Derrick Rose, the Bulls' bone-china star, leaves early in the second half with a sprained ankle—and the Cavs, with a road trip next week for games in Portland, Salt Lake City, and Denver, want that first W, as do I. I still don't like it. All during preseason, LeBron talked about needing to play fewer minutes, to preserve his body, and David Blatt seemed amenable. Then the season started.

After the win, the players gathers around Blatt, and LeBron hands him the game ball and gives him a hug; the team mobs him, mussing his hair and hooting as men who shower together do. When Blatt meets the media, he lets them in on the key to victory—David Blatt.

"You all are such nice people, I'm so happy you weren't in the morning meeting today because your opinion of me might be vastly different right now," he says.

Ah. The Eurocoach was so dismayed by last night's loss to the Knicks that instead of a morning shootaround, he gave his team holy hell at a breakfast meeting at their hotel. And it's clearly vital to the new coach that the media understand its pivotal importance.

"We cleaned some things up, and the guys responded beautifully, and we played a great game."

Jesus. It's bizarre for any NBA coach to hold a meeting the morning after the season's first game to ream his team; bragging about it to the media is foolish, grandiose. Asked about the postgame celebration, Blatt doubles down.

"You know the funny thing about that is, not all of you

know me that well, but I've probably won about seven hundred games in my career—just none of them have been here. So it was a little bit odd on one hand, but that's the first NBA game and that's a bit of history for my friends and my family—and I'm glad I did it with the Cleveland Cavaliers."

Vey iz mir. Number one, I'd bet my house that David Blatt knows precisely how many games he's won. The exact number. No doubt in my mind that you could wake him at any hour and he'd be eager to share with you his winning percentage, broken down season by season.

Number two, Princeton, shminceton: What a putz. His Eurowins don't mean jackshit, not here, not to the media, not to LeBron, and certainly not to me. But instead of showing excitement and pleasure after his first coaching win in the world's best league by far, instead of expressing his delight and gratitude for his players' goodwill, Blatt seems both pompous and defensive.

I don't think he understands these things, any more than I think he understands the kind of men he's being paid more than $3 million per year to coach.

All of this is new to him, I know. But at least he should have grasped by now that the Cavs job he signed up for no longer exists. Now, he's coaching LeBron and the second-highest payroll in NBA history. Now, he's coaching a team expected to win it all. For the next nine months, the daily media scrutiny will be granular. His arrogance tonight will read as weakness by the reporters, local and national, assigned to cover the Cavs—all hungry for copy, searching for angles, tweeting links to each note of discord. To them, Blatt's just one more glazed donut in a blue suit.

Worse, by trumpeting his mastery first, he's telling the best basketball players alive that he's the one who matters most to him. By trivializing their celebration of the win, Blatt's displaying his own detachment and disrespect for them at an unstable, precarious time. Shake up any human structure, any family, any workplace, any yoga class, and people get shook. Earning authority and trust in an NBA locker room full of rich young African Americans is a far cry from coaching Benetton Treviso and Aris Thessaloniki. And however dazzling David Blatt's schematic wizardry may be, it won't matter if he won't reduce LeBron's workload. Come the playoffs, it will make no difference whether Blatt's bloated ego is 100 percent healthy unless LeBron's back and knees are, too.

Forty minutes? Give me ten, and I'll drill some sense through Blatt's thick skull and thin skin. We'd start with Malamud, of course—not *The Natural*, the subject of his thesis, but *The Assistant*, where the grocer Morris Bober works and suffers in noble constraint, one more Jew martyred by roughneck goyim. I know I can help this Jew. Look what I did for LeBron.

THE BEST PART OF the Cavs' win is Judah and me parked in the Liberty Bell driveway, listening to the comeback and overtime on the car radio, eating McFlurries—dinner was

Five Guys, no culinary sin—cheering each bucket. This—this kid, this love, this joy—is worth five grand, easy. It's all cliché. Even listening to the game on the car radio feels goofy to me. But not to him. He's never done it. And this may be the biggest Cleveland win we've ever enjoyed together—I can't remember, so I ask him.

"Giambi's home run last season," Judah says.

He's right. Late last September, forty-two-year-old Jason Giambi hauled his fat ass off the Tribe bench with two outs in the bottom of the ninth after the Indians' closer blew a lead and blasted a two-run shot to win a game that helped nail down a wild-card slot. We watched that on TV. One week later, we drove to Cleveland for the one-game play-in, saw the Tribe get shut out, and drove all night to get him back to school on time.

Does it truly matter if the Cavs win? Fuck yes. AND not really, not if he remembers Giambi's homer, not if this is what still binds us now. I used to read Whitman to him when he was inside the womb. I know that humans are born loving rhythm, music, poetry, and I know that life will murder that love dead if you let it. He likes Yeats better now, because when we visit Ireland, we always stop for a piss at Thoor Ballylee, Yeats's old Galway castle, and visit his grave in Sligo, beneath Ben Bulben. I spared him Delmore Schwartz and Sylvia Plath in favor of Robert Pinsky and Gerry Stern—happy, relatively speaking, Jews.

I fed him Chuck Jones, too, and Popeye, early Spielberg and Kubrick, Monk and Mingus, Robert Johnson and John

Lee. But the souls of the old, fretful Jew and the fresh half-breed weren't going to meld over yesteryear. *Sports.* He was a player from the start—like his mother and her brothers, good athletes—and he was hard on himself right away. Kids start organized sports in this town when they're five or six, which is insane. Fathers brag about how football is teaching their little boys to compete.

Judah knew. He worked. Lisa went one-on-one with him for hours in the dining room; we had a small hoop hung on the kitchen door. He played baseball and basketball all the way up—he never wanted to play football, and we wouldn't have let him. I would've preferred reading as a leisure-time pursuit. I worried about injuries. Even a floor burn could turn to staph overnight. Now it's soccer, and I shout "No headers!" from the bleachers whenever he heads the ball. And Judah looks at me and shrugs or glares, depending on the score, and plays his game.

I'm good with that. That's my son out there, not me, and he goes hard. Win or lose—and once Glen Ridge teams start traveling to other, bigger, less pale towns, we most often lose—all that matters is that I'm here, and that we are . . .

Together on three. Hard work on six.

God *DAMN* it. I interviewed Dan Wieden once, back when Wieden + Kennedy was a young agency so hot that they won the Subaru account, a huge coup. W+K opened an office in Philly to handle the work, and I wrote a feature story for *Philadelphia* magazine trashing their campaign rollout—"What To Drive," it was called, and it was complete crapola—and Wieden called me, mad as hell.

"You're either a schizophrenic or the biggest asshole I've ever met," he said.

I tell Judah the story.

"Well," he says, "you're not schizophrenic."

God bless sports. God save Cleveland. God keep LeBron James.

9

CHILL MODE (PART I)

Things fall apart fast. In Portland, the Cavs open by hitting their first ten shots, but when the Blazers punch back, they fall apart. No effort on defense. No ball movement on offense. Kyrie gets torched by Damian Lillard and hits but three of seventeen shots; he and Dion spend the second half dribbling endlessly while LeBron strolls to the corner and stands beyond the three-point arc watching them playing one-on-one as the shot clock winds down. The Cavs score thirty-four points in the first quarter, forty-eight total in the last three, and lose 101-82. LeBron scores eleven points, none in the second half, when Irving and Waiters combine for nineteen shots to LeBron's four.

No passing. No cutting. And afterward, no Kyrie, who skips without speaking to the press. LeBron, on the other hand, has plenty to say.

"It's going to be a long process, man. There's been a lot of losing basketball around here for a few years. There's a lot of bad habits—a lot of bad habits have been built up over the last couple of years, and when you play that style of basketball it takes a lot to get it up out of you.

"Everyone wants to win, I would hope. Would you rather play selfish basketball and lose, or play unselfish basketball and sacrifice and win—you pick it. A lot of the guys that are going to help us win ultimately haven't played a lot of meaningful basketball games in our league. But I'm here to help, and that's what it's about."

This guy. Goes to Miami for four years, wins a couple of rings, and now he's Dr. fucking Phil. Not that LeBron's wrong: Over the last two seasons, led by Kyrie and Dion, the Cavs' win-loss record is 57-107. At a players-only meeting early last season—the Cavs were 4-11 at the time—Dion bitched about Kyrie playing "buddy ball" with Tristan Thompson instead of passing to him, and things escalated to the point where players had to keep Dion and Tristan from throwing punches. Then Dion complained to the coach and the general manager that Kyrie got to stay in games when he played like crap, whereas "Kobe Wade" got benched.

Three games into the new season, little has changed between Dion and Kyrie, whose father played pro ball and sent him to private high schools followed by a single, injury-shortened year at Duke. And even with LeBron and his old-head cadre—not to mention the rookie head coach who made his bones coaching players hauling down seventy grand a year plus free rent on an apartment in lovely Novgorod—the Cavs' locker room isn't big enough for this nonsense.

I could help Dion, too. Give me five minutes. I lived in

Philly for five years, met Lisa there, got married at City Hall. To Dion, I'd speak the language of brotherly love: Get your head out of your ass, pal. Kyrie isn't just an All-Star, he's already Pepsi's Uncle Drew; the coach who wanted you—Byron Scott craved Dion, which is why the Cavs blew a fourth-in-the-nation pick on a player they never interviewed before the draft—was fired two seasons ago; and, oh, by the way, if you'd stop pounding the rock long enough to look up, you might spot LeBron James wearing the same uniform, drifting in the corner, staring at you while you pretend you're a star. Pass, play hard on defense, shut the fuck up, and you may get a ring and respect—because guess what? The Cavaliers tried to trade your showboat head-case ass last year, and found no takers.

Blatt, meanwhile, is already roadkill. Three games in, LeBron's speaking frankly to the media about the Cavs' culture in the voice of a veteran head coach, not a superstar leader who spent much of the game as an on-court bystander, watching his team get drubbed.

Eleven points from LeBron? Cool with Blatt.

"I don't hold him responsible. We have to help get him looks. It's not only about him. It's about helping him get looks."

Genius.

On the bright side, LeBron plays only thirty-five minutes, Kevin Love puts up another double-double, and Blatt enjoys a reunion with Portland's head coach, who visited Blatt in Istanbul a few years back, to pick his fecund brain.

"Obviously," says Blatt, "one of the best ways to learn is to observe and to inquire and to share ideas with other great coaches."

I've got an idea worth sharing, coach: rent, don't buy.

THE BEST NEWS OF the day is that Glen Ridge votes down artificial turf, for the third time. In a borough with 1.5 square miles of land, a median annual household income of 160 grand, and no shortage of entitlement, a contingent of alpha dads accustomed to the fealty of their underlings at the firm are pissed off because their progeny might be deprived of a partial lacrosse scholarship at some Division II school if they're forced to play on overused grass fields—and having been voted down twice, their attitude is why don't you morons see that *we're only thinking of what's best for the children?*

Judah played a hard-nosed center back on the junior-varsity soccer team this season—his teammates voted him Mister Defense—and when he arose from a tackle in a late-season match on a turf field in West Orange, his lower right leg looked like someone had put a blowtorch to it. I cleaned, dressed, bandaged, and prayed over the oozing wound daily for three weeks until it finally scabbed. You can afford full tuition, you Bluetoothed pricks—fuck you and fuck your turf.

Families here hire au pairs, drive BMW SUVs, and own dogs whose teeth cleanings cost seven hundred bucks. We took Pip to a vet in Upper Montclair who drew $200 worth of blood to treat an ear infection and wanted to put him on a daily thyroid pill forever.

What? He's a mutt. He's healthy. He eats dirt.

"He lacks hybrid vigor."

So we found another vet.

Property taxes are fourteen grand a year. The country club costs another bundle if you join, which we don't. On Halloween, the kids from East Orange ring the doorbell for white-people candy. Their brothers swipe our kids' bikes. Our cops make a surprising number of stops involving drivers of color on Ridgewood Avenue—surprising if you're oblivious to the permanent race war in America.

You're oblivious only if you truly wish to be. Surely you're aware of the gaps in the bare facts of existence—life expectancy, poverty, educational attainment, employment—in this country. And if you are aware, which is to say if you are sentient, you have chosen one of two overarching, mutually exclusive explanations for the huge disparities: Either America remains largely defined by a racist culture or those others must be inferior, ill bred, and inherently unfit. They enjoy the same rights, opportunities, and challenges as white folks. They're just not good enough.

I don't bring this up to prove my humanist bona fides as a white man writing about a black man in America, but because I have no bona fides. My last memorable personal interaction with a black man was thirty years ago, at the Jewish nursing home where I was the only white employee at night. I had the key to a small office in the basement, where I smoked weed with the orderlies, and one of them looked at me one night, red eyed, dead serious, and said, "You know, I always thought I would get married to a white woman," and I looked at him and said, "Me, too."

Race was an issue in *The Whore of Akron*, too. It's a clumsy subject for white people, fraught with guilt, denial, and ignorance. I love subjects like that, and this one is my very favorite. You ever ask yourself why Jews built Hollywood, or why blacks dominate sports in America, or why so many Irish became cops and politicians?

Simple: they had few other options for success in a nation where the most powerful tribe achieved primacy by slaughtering the indigenous and enslaving the African, believing all the while that their special God was fine with that because those were subhuman beings. Demonized, shunned, ghettoized, they went where the jobs were, or built lives from scratch, or fought their way out.

First-generation Jews from the New York City tenements won boxing titles; Jewish hoopers ruled the city's pro and college teams in the 1930s to such an extent that a *Daily News* columnist came up with a theory that "the game appeals to the Hebrew with his Oriental background. The game places a premium on an alert, scheming mind, flashy trickiness, artful dodging, and general smartalecness."

Of course. And poor blacks with no formal training created new genres of American music of indelible beauty and unmatched power—and still do—because darkies have rhythm. And big dicks.

I've always been impressed by the efforts white people make to buttress their frail sense of difference and superiority—muscle-fiber studies, slave-breeding theories, IQ-test analysis, Larry Bird fan clubs. The meaning of the color of human skin is such an inexplicable mystery, as bewildering as Thomas Jefferson's four-decade, six-child shadow marriage to his slave Sally Hemings. Or not. It could be that Jefferson fell in love, and the only true mystery is why it's so hard to accept the glaring truth: human passion, intelligence, and talent are not bestowed according to any forced, false construct of monolithic racial, religious, or ethnic groups.

That's what "all men are created equal" means. Limit the number of places where men can take their talent, intelligence, and passion, and you'll find a lot of driven, gifted men in those places.

The particular beauty of major sports in America is that they are huge businesses and, as such, true equal-opportunity employers, by far the most visible and visibly integrated workplaces in the nation over the seventy years since 1947, when Jackie Robinson and Larry Doby broke baseball's color barrier—eight years before Rosa Parks's arrest in Montgomery.

Sports are still the main stage for American race relations in vivo. Sports is where, fifty years after Jim Brown spoke of dignity, Richard Sherman has to deconstruct the word *thug* for the media, while guys like me parse the meaning of LeBron and a locker room culture we'll never truly know.

I went at it sideways writing *The Whore of Akron*. I have no black friends, editors, or colleagues. Every lengthy conversation I've had with black men for the past thirty years was an interview with some actor, director, stand-up comic, or pro athlete. I tried reaching out to African American men whose writing I knew—Ta-Nehisi Coates, Bill Rhoden, John Edgar Wideman, others—and each of them kindly, wisely declined to speak on the record about LeBron James and my animus toward him, and what it might mean.

I don't know what I don't know about growing up in any tribal culture other than my own, but I do know this: I know that I'm a Jew every second of my life. It defines everything I do and think, beyond religious practice. It makes me *me*, and to a large extent, makes me feel like an outsider in my own land. Men being men, I figure that African American men, including LeBron James, feel more intensely so.

And as for dignity, what the hell. At least I didn't call it "The Ho of Akron." *Whore* was a Book of Revelations reference, and a tip of the yarmulke to Woody's "The Whore of Mensa," a great short story. And, of course, a profound insult to my hero's manhood and morals, courtesy of a fat Jew sitting at a keyboard in New Jersey.

THEY'RE TRYING TO KILL me, I swear. The night after Portland, they lose to the Jazz. Dion's on the bench; Shawn Marion is the starting off-guard. Blatt bastes LeBron for forty-two minutes, in a back-to-back on a road trip, and he again looks lifeless until, with seventeen seconds left and the Cavs down four, he nails a three, gets fouled on another attempt, and hits all three free throws to knot the game at 100 with three seconds left. Then Utah hits a jumper at the buzzer, and the Cavs are now 1-3.

Kyrie finishes as the game's leading scorer with thirty-four points and an astonishing zero assists in forty-five minutes. ZERO assists. None. Free of Dion waving and yelping for the ball, oblivious to the offense Blatt wishes him to run, the Cavs' point guard never once finds a way to pass the ball from his own hands into the hands of any teammate, including LeBron James, who, upon receiving said pass, scores a basket.

As a team, the Cavs register a total of six assists on thirty made baskets, tying the franchise record set in 1970, their year of birth, when the team won fifteen games all season. In fact, *no* NBA team has managed so few assists for an entire game since 2010. If this was Kyrie responding to LeBron's dig about selfish play and bad habits, it was a splendid fuck-you.

"No, no, no," says Kyrie. "I knew they were trusting me with the ball—I know Bron was trusting me with the ball, as well as the rest of the team. We have great players on this team. We gave guys ample opportunities—guys just weren't hitting."

Zero assists. Zero.

"Sometimes things happen in the game, and you have to take it. Me and Bron saw that at the end of the game."

What LeBron saw was a loss:

"There's no way you're going to win a basketball game like that, just having six assists. We can't win like that, and we've got to figure out a way to help each other and not make it so tough."

And in the locker room after the game, LeBron told Kyrie, "You can never have another game with no assists. You can have just one, two, three, but you can't have zero."

"All right," Kyrie said. "Cool. It won't happen again."

The next day, LeBron tweets, "In the words of the great @AaronRodgers12 'RELAX.'"

To which I can only subtweet, "Have you never met a Jew?"

SEVENTY-EIGHT GAMES UNTIL THE playoffs. I have no idea what's up with LeBron. The media ask about his lower back, and he says, "I'm in the lineup. I'm good." But his bursts of speed are few and he gets out-quicked too often going to the rim. His outside shot looks awful, and except for the Bulls game, he hasn't looked much like prime King James, and hasn't looked like he much cares. No one is playing hard defense, they're getting out-rebounded, and it seems like David Blatt and LeBron James have yet to discuss much but the weather.

The media has noticed. They ask LeBron whether he consulted Blatt about calling out the Cavs' bad habits and selfish play.

Nah.

"I don't look for his guidance," LeBron says. "I just spoke what I believe in and what I think will help our team in the long run."

Blatt sent his own message by benching Dion, who reacted to the demotion by not coming out of the locker room for the national anthem. Blatt tells the press he hasn't yet seen LeBron's comments—bullshit pure—but being David Blatt, he also has to fill them in on his own strategy for schooling the young Cavs.

"You got kids? I got four. I taught a lot of them. You watch. You show. You speak. You use examples. You hug. You never hit. But you do admonish. How's that?"

Great. NBA players *love* when the bossman likens them to children. David Blatt, David *Blatt*, DAVID *BLATT.* The poor dog jerks awake. He's wearing a plastic cone around his neck to keep him from gnawing on what the new vet calls a granuloma—an open sore on his right forepaw. One hundred and ninety-two dollars. She threw in the cone, free.

I worry about LeBron, about Blatt, about LeBron and Blatt. I don't worry about Kyrie Irving. I believe in Kyrie Irving. I remember what the Cavs locker room felt like during the last year of LeBron's first tour of duty with Cleveland: Everyone deferred to King James, including the husk of Shaq, twenty-one million clams' worth of who-gives-a-fuck. There, wrapped in a towel by the double-wide corner locker, young LeBron held court. Some things haven't changed: Old LeBron's ego is titanic, his primacy assumed. He knows that he remains the best basketball player in the world.

Kyrie Irving, however, knows that Kyrie Irving is the best basketball player in the world, and unlike Dion, who knows that Dion Waiters is the best basketball player in the world,

Kyrie knows he has the game to back the claim. After he won the league's Rookie of the Year award, Kyrie scrimmaged against the US Olympic team back in 2012, and when Kobe Bryant talked shit, Kyrie challenged Kobe to play him one-on-one. Bryant told him to call his daddy for permission first. Irving ragged Bryant about his defense. They agreed on a duel after the season for fifty grand, before Kobe tore his Achilles.

That's the guy LeBron needs to win a championship, and LeBron knows it. They'll figure it out. It's only November 5, and the Cavs have a ten-day, five-game home stand coming up on both sides of Thanksgiving. I'll bring my mojo. The Browns are 5-3, and the town is going nuts. Cleveland fans are far more fanatical about the Browns than the Cavs or the Tribe, and, given the state of the team, far angrier. Pro football is a vicious sport, a brutalizing enterprise that ruins the men who play it, and tosses them away like so much trash, and by God if the Brownies are 5-3, count me in. Tomorrow night they're playing the Bengals in Cincinnati, on national TV.

LISA CONVERTED TO CLEVELAND sports, too. It must be love. She's cultured. She has a grad degree in film, another in journalism. We have thousands of books—she could read, or walk the dog, or hit a movie instead of watching ball games. She's nearing sixty now herself, and came of age when sisterhood was powerful. Never worn makeup—never even pierced her ears. I know she's beautiful. She must love me, because she's watching Cleveland sports. She was waiting, approaching forty when we met, my trophy wife.

No disrespect meant to my first wife. She was a fan, too. She grew up on the West Side—we met at Cleveland State. Sports were the only thing I ever talked about with her father, who barely spoke. Instead, he'd grin or nod. He grew up in an orphanage in Montana, half Crow, half Northern Cheyenne, and worked as a grill cook. I don't think he'd ever met a Jew before. Maybe in the army.

First wife and I saw Cleveland teams play all over the country—if I shut my eyes, I can still see Bernie Kosar almost getting his throwing arm ripped off in Kansas City in 1988—and I never went behind her back until I met Lisa.

It was *Barfly* for a while, but Lisa and I got better and we've been together more than twenty years now. I don't know why. What passes for love has grown simpler for me over the years: You take care of each other, even at your worst. You ride it out. You jump in the car and drive to Atlantic City, drop two or three hundred, and you look at the waitresses and the customers and your face in the men's room mirror, and you know what Sandy Raab would do, so you do the other thing: Jump in the car, go home, and say I'm sorry and I love you.

I don't know what it says about me that both my wives like Cleveland sports and touching corpses. My first wife specialized in pathology; I watched her do postmortems during residency. Lisa is part of a synagogue group that practices *tahara*, an ancient Hebrew purification ritual, washing the freshly dead before burial. I wouldn't enter a hot tub without an infectious disease specialist, and she's in a *mikvah* cleansing a naked stiff. This, according to Lisa, is a deeply emotional and spiritual experience, which, as far as I remember, an autopsy was not.

The naked and the dead. Both wives. It must mean something, but what?

I make a mental note to move more during sex. Quicken the pace. Share the ball. Get the whole team involved. Energy. Pressure on D. Make her *feel* you. Because what we do tonight is gonna define what we're about.

One, two, three, *NO MAN!*

Four, five, six, *IS AUTHOR OF HIS FATE!*

But once in a while, it's good not to dwell on it. There's more to life than work, sports, and death. There must also be a pregame dinner. Turkey meatloaf. Tabouleh. A protein bar. On TV trays. There will be popcorn, of which the dog is especially fond, at the half.

The Browns drub the Bengals. They now have six wins in the first nine games of a sixteen-game season. The Browns haven't won six games over the course of an entire season since 2007, four head coaches ago. Already this season, they've whipped both the Bengals and the Steelers, bitter division and historical rivals, and now sit atop the AFC North.

The Cavs, thank goodness, have the evening off.

OVER THEIR NEXT EIGHT games, the Cavs win four straight, then lose four straight. In the wins, their offense is a machine averaging nearly 120 points per game; in the losses, they average not quite ninety. In both the wins and the losses, they play lethargic defense, lose focus for long stretches on offense. They give up large leads or fall behind by big margins, sometimes in the same game, and let LeBron author their fate. If he carries the load, the Cavs win; if not, they lose.

Most nights they get little offense from their bench, and, win or lose, Blatt rides the starters hard. Before the fourth consecutive win, the media asks about LeBron's minutes, and Blatt tells the press, "He's feeling good and he's starting to feel he's in game shape—so this is not the time to be thinking about resting him. This is the time to allow him to feel comfortable and get into his rhythm."

That night, the Cavs nail their first eleven three-point shots, score seventy-one first-half points, share the basketball to the tune of thirty-nine assists on forty-nine made baskets, play hard defense, and maul the Hawks, 127-94. LeBron scores thirty-two points in his twenty-nine minutes. Two nights later, after missing that morning's shootaround with a head cold, he plays forty-one ugly minutes in a loss to the Denver Nuggets, winners of two of their first nine games.

"We just didn't come with the proper mind-set," Blatt says after the loss, "or with the energy level we had the last several games."

The media then asks LeBron about what Blatt just told them, and LeBron says, "It's easy to say that after the fact—I didn't feel it."

The next morning, LeBron informs the media that he's

playing too many minutes. In fact, Blatt's Big Three rank third, fourth, and fifth in the NBA in minutes played per game. Led by LeBron.

"For me, I don't want to do that all year. Obviously right now it's difficult, because we're trying to find a groove, and we're trying to find a rhythm, and we're trying to find something that you can't shortcut. But at the same time you gotta be smart about it."

Blatt's dumb, but not that dumb.

"It might be a good idea," Blatt says after practice, "for our guys to play shorter stretches harder, rather than longer stretches. We're going to see how we can incorporate that philosophy."

Poorly is how. Sadly is how. In the next game, against the Spurs, the Cavs lose, 92-90. LeBron plays only thirty-four minutes, hits only six of seventeen shots, and loses the ball with two seconds left in the game, costing the Cavs a chance to tie or win.

But it's Blatt who screws the pooch: He loses track of his rotations throughout the game, and keeps Irving, Love, and LeBron on the bench for the last two minutes of the third quarter while San Antonio surges ahead. In the fourth quarter, Blatt burns three time-outs in less than a minute, leaving LeBron unable to call time on the game's final play, rather than rush downcourt to force a miracle.

This is David Blatt's first real test as an NBA head coach—facing the defending NBA champions and their Hall of Fame head coach, Greg Popovich—and Blatt falls flat on his face.

TWO MORE LOSSES FOLLOW, along with fresh woe: Kevin Love has lost his way in the Cavs' offense. Of course he has: I've seen this movie before, in Miami, with LeBron, Wade, and Chris Bosh. It is an Xs and Os issue—LeBron and Kyrie, the primary ball handlers and scorers, need lanes to the basket; Love down low on offense draws a crowd, and unless a play is drawn specifically to get the ball to him near the basket, he generally hangs behind the three-point line, spotting up in case of a drive-and-kick to him from Irving or James.

But it's also an ego issue, because organizations are complex human systems, and this team is a traveling men's group. In lieu of a therapist, they yak at the media—LeBron especially, which is a huge change from his first go-round as a Cavalier, when he gradually, and in the end completely, froze out the media, starting with the locals.

And believe me, not for nothing. Teenage LeBron was already the most famous athlete in Northeast Ohio, and it wasn't a romance: there was a proud, loud, black mother who'd lived a tough life; there was LeBron driving a leased Hummer to school, and an investigation into the ownership thereof; in his senior year, the state high school athletic association handed him a season-long suspension for taking two throwback jerseys from a sporting-goods store in exchange for posing for photos the store hung on the wall, followed by a lawsuit that overturned the suspension.

The national press drooled over the Chosen One stuff: Shaq visiting Akron to watch him play; Michael inviting him to his summer camp; the shoe-company bidding war ending with LeBron signed to a seven-year, $90 million Nike deal before the draft. The locals covered all that and the hard stuff, too, day after day after day, and LeBron hadn't forgotten. As his first seven seasons with the Cavs all ended with loss instead of a ring, failure became the focus, the heart of every postseason obit and team preview.

There was a rough patch in 2007, when LeBron showed up at the Jake in a fucking Yankees cap for the opener of a playoff series between New York and the Tribe in 2007. He caught vicious, righteous shit for that, a clot of which I tossed. And his year of villainy in Miami—and especially the night of his first return to the Q with the Heat—inspired operatic hate broadcast around the world and live on the road every game. He endured it, learned from it, surmounted it.

He won. He's back. This Moses doesn't stutter. LeBron holds forth on a near-daily basis, shepherding his power. However well he plays on any night, whatever he tells teammates and coaches in meetings and the locker room, LeBron's also using the media, especially social media, to guide his flocks and turn some coin. One and all—players, press, fans, and front office—we hang on every tweet. It's King James's odyssey—not David Blatt's or Dan Gilbert's—and LeBron knows it.

I don't know or care why LeBron didn't deign to meet with Blatt sooner during the summer, or why he and the team aren't playing harder, smarter, more consistent ball. Fortunately, they boast more talent than any other team in the Eastern Conference by a mile, and a whole season to figure out how to deploy it.

What I worry about is what I believe LeBron's worried about—his game, his body, the only equity he truly has. He's not right—not as quick, not as strong, not as far above the rim—not Peak LeBron. After eleven seasons in the NBA, he understands his body, *feels* the minutes he's playing, knows the hurt and fatigue—physical, mental, spiritual—that build over eighty-two regular-season games and ten weeks of play-offs.

LeBron also knows the Cavs have been a shit show for four seasons and what Blatt's Eurowins are worth. He began preaching patience in his homecoming essay—"We're not ready right now. No way. Of course, I want to win next year, but I'm realistic. It will be a long process, much longer than it was in 2010"—and while I didn't buy it, then or now, it was, as usual, the smart play.

Blatt has no leverage beyond a three-year contract, which, given Dan Gilbert's history, is worth less than a square of Charmin, and he has no power beyond controlling LeBron's playing time. Blatt clearly can't afford patience or questions about his authority, or he wouldn't feel the need to blow up at the team on the morning after Opening Night and tell the press about it. Blatt's not trying to install his quicker, cutting offense to force LeBron to play harder, nor is he burning him forty minutes a game as punishment. David Blatt, unlike LeBron, needs to win each game. That's the only authority he has.

Blatt, unlike LeBron, can't play offense against the media, and he has never had to play D. Because of LeBron, the Cavs are an easy lay for any dangling wee dick posed at a typepad or microphone. The obvious story—Can He Work Well with LeBron?—presumes his role as the Fall Guy and LeBron's as his nemesis, because Blatt, unlike LeBron, is easy to replace.

The media covering the Cavs are smart and experienced. They're the A team, working the most visible beat in the league—and they didn't have to play football to learn to compete any more than you or I did. Their job often sucks. Like the players, they're on the road, away from home and family, living out of a suitcase. They are paid well by middle-class standards, but peons to the players, or worse. When one reporter asked Dion Waiters why he didn't show up on court for the national anthem against Utah—the night Blatt gave Shawn Marion Dion's starter's job—Dion came out as a Muslim by way of explaining that his pregame prayer ritual had run a little long, triggering three full days of controversy, clumsy clarifications, and a Cleveland.com column that reminds fans that Blatt's a Jew, and that Waiters's revelation could spark fan backlash—you know, "given the United States' decades of military battles in the Middle East and the attacks against Americans on Sept. 11, 2001 and Sept. 11, 2012 (at the American embassy in Libya)."

Okay, they're not all smart. But they're all good at taking quotes from Blatt to LeBron, and from LeBron to Blatt. And now they've got Love sharing his feelings, too.

"I'm just trying to find myself in this offense," Love says after the loss to the Spurs; Love scored ten points and rarely touched the ball after the first quarter. "I'm just trying to find different spots. I'm not worried about it. I'm not mad, and I don't feel any sort of grudge or anything like that. I just want to help this team. We're going to be okay. It's still early."

He's not wrong—he was the Timberwolves' only prayer every game of his entire career, and now he's number three—four, if you're asking Dion—but that quote is one more story line of woe, and I've had enough. More than enough. Fifty years of enough.

I find myself once more facing a truth too familiar, a truth I've had to swallow countless times over the years as a Cleveland fan: I don't like this team. They're not playing hard—Love and Irving are terrible defenders, swinging doors—and still early or no, I'm pissed off. I can't abide their struggling with any more grace than my own. If they're not giving 110 percent every nanosecond of every game, they're trash. As a fan, I can't grant them humanity in full, and they aren't merely a story. They're the scrim for my own rage and impotence.

Get a fucking grip, man. It wasn't Cleveland sports that broke me, and a championship won't heal me. LeBron is not author of my fate. Blatt's maybe, but not mine. Forget about Thanksgiving in Cleveland. I'm not going to spend it at the Liberty Bell, alone with a Circle K Southwest Chicken Wrap and a Coke Zero. I'm not insane.

10

CHILL MODE (PART II)

I find out about Tamir Rice the morning after the Cavs lose at home by seventeen to the Raptors, a good young team with an 11-2 win-loss record. The Cavs are 5-7.

"We're a very fragile team right now," LeBron says afterward. "We were a fragile team from the beginning. Any little adversity that hits us, we just shell up."

I noticed, Bron. Everyone's noticing everything all the time.

That's Saturday night.

Saturday afternoon, Tamir, a twelve-year-old boy, was shot by a rookie Cleveland cop near a gazebo at a West Side recreation center. The 911 caller said the gun he saw Tamir fooling with was likely a fake—it was—and that Tamir was likely a juvenile, but when the squad car rolled up on him, the cop came out firing, and two seconds later, Tamir Rice lay dying.

Monday night comes word that no indictment was returned in Ferguson for Michael Brown's killing in August. LeBron Instagrams a cartoon of Brown and Trayvon Martin walking, one arm hooked over the other's shoulder, into eternity's white light. The next day, asked about the subsequent protests in Ferguson, he is as cautious as any sane and famous man of any color would be, offers his thoughts and prayers, discourages violence, and leaves it there.

What else, what more, can or should he say? This isn't 1964; he isn't Jim Brown or Ali. He speaks for the Cavaliers, for McDonald's, for Nike; he is the father of young black sons; he has come to refer back to his own young inner-city self as "a statistic that should have gone the other way." Who am I to judge his public reaction? He can't save Cleveland by himself, let alone heal America.

I have nothing at stake, and little to say beyond the obvious: for each bad-apple cop in the country who kills a young black man, two or three or twenty more—along with the prosecutors shielding them—seem to find comfort in complicity. Anyhow, I'm busy with a story about the billionaires, bureaucrats, and politicians who've made 9/11 into a bottomless public-funded honeypot. I've got a Will Smith cover story coming up. I'll just ask Will what he thinks about race relations in America these days. That should do it.

WINTER COMES AND CHANGES nothing for the better. The Browns peak at 7-4, then drop their last five games. Johnny Manziel gets a couple of starts and shits the bed. The season ends as most Browns seasons do, in disgrace, with Johnny and his fellow first-round draft pick, Justin Gilbert, suspended by the team for the last game of the season. So far, the traditional firing of the coach has been deferred.

The season's highlight wasn't a play or a game; it came before Manziel's first start, when the Browns' receiver Andrew Hawkins wore a black T-shirt onto the field for warmups before a home game versus Cincinnati, with huge white letters reading JUSTICE FOR TAMIR RICE AND JOHN CRAWFORD!!! on the front, and THE REAL BATTLE FOR OHIO on the back. John Crawford was a twenty-two-year-old black man, shot dead by police in August inside a southern Ohio Walmart because he was holding an air rifle. No indictment was returned.

The Cavs get a chance to don protest T-shirts before a December game against the Nets in Brooklyn, a few days after a New York grand jury brings no criminal charges against the New York City policeman who killed Eric Garner in July with a choke hold banned by the NYPD in 1993. LeBron and Kyrie sport I CAN'T BREATHE tees for the pregame shootaround, as do many of the Nets.

"Obviously, as a society we have to do better," LeBron says. "We have to be better for one another. It doesn't matter what race you are. It's more of a shout-out to the family, because they're the ones that should be getting all the energy and effort. It's not a Cavs thing. It's a worldly thing."

That's right. Prince William is in the house, with his missus. Commisioner Adam Silver, too.

"I respect all of our players for voicing their personal views on important issues but my preference would be for players to abide by our on-court attire rules," Silver says.

Of course. Adidas, not justice, pays the NBA $400 million a year to provide the official apparel of the NBA, and these uppities had their logos covered. In a gesture of magnanimous solidarity, the commissioner issues no fines for these violations. The Browns, too, stand tall when Cleveland's police union boss demands an apology for Hawkins's Tamir T-shirt, offering its corporate respect to the cops and "our players' rights to project their support and bring awareness to issues that are important to them if done so in a responsible manner."

All this seems preposterous to me. I don't believe I'll ever witness a Cleveland sports championship, and yet I thought that electing Barack Obama would soothe America's racist soul. I should have known better. I turned sixteen the summer Dr. King and Bobby Kennedy were gunned down, and by then I'd already experienced a president's assassination, and annual urban uprisings answered with military force and body counts that would do Daesh proud. I'd seen Jews like Mailer and Leonard Bernstein fetishize the Black Panthers, and I'd seen J. Edgar Hoover dispatch death squads to kill them.

Fifty years later, we're all watching surveillance and cell phone footage of black men being murdered by cops— lynchings broadcast worldwide and legalized post facto by prosecutors. Protest is met by tanks again, just as in the olden days, and black athletes wearing T-shirts asking for justice get pats on the head.

I'm a catastrophist by trade and inclination, an aging Jew

crankier by the day, but I have never had to teach my son—
who sees the footage, too—that, plan or no, any traffic stop,
any wrong move, any move at all, might end with him shot
dead.

STILL WAITING ON RECONSTRUCTION'S promise, the Cavs pull
out of Brooklyn on a seven-win streak, which lifts their record up to 12-7. Two days later, LeBron sits out with a sore
knee, and they lose. He comes back the following night and
drops forty-one points in thirty-eight minutes, and they lose
again, 119-114, allowing a New Orleans team playing without Anthony Davis, injured six minutes in, to score at will.
Two games later, at the Q, they lose to Atlanta 127-98, in so
effortless a manner that David Blatt is moved to brevity.

"I don't want to get up and walk out of here," he tells the
media postgame. "That's not fair to you people, but I don't
have too much to say."

Right there would have been an excellent place for Blatt to
stop, but that's not David Blatt. He enjoys parrying with the
media. Perhaps he finds comfort in the back-and-forth, some
vestige of the prestige once accorded him in other parts of
the world, or maybe he's just grateful that anyone is paying
attention to anything he says. Whatever the case, he can't
stop his tongue.

"But I will say this: that was embarrassing, how we played.
I apologize to all the good fans who came out here, as they
always do."

The first poor beat reporter who carries Blatt's "embarrassing" message over to LeBron gets the skunk eye.

"Do you only ask negative questions?" LeBron snaps.

Once it's clear that Blatt himself used that word, LeBron's demeanor doesn't change.

"Nah," he says. "I'm embarrassed losing the Finals."

Me, I'm embarrassed to still give an actual shit. Sundays, I'm watching the Browns lose on a pirate website; the stream is free, but the cost to my soul can be measured by the slabs of turkey loaf on my dinner plate. The Cavaliers are worse. They have talent, but it is impossible to ignore Blatt's growing pains—by now, it's apparent that LeBron prefers talking to Blatt's assistant, Tyronn Lue, hired by Dan Gilbert along with Blatt, paid the highest salary ever for an NBA assistant and granted the title "associate head coach" because "plan B" would've been too obvious.

It's also impossible to ignore the drop-off in LeBron's game, and the media doesn't hesitate to ask.

"You can look at it in a bad way or a good way. I've expanded the rest of my game. I'm still out there making plays. My athleticism—obviously I'm not the eighteen-year-old kid that I was before, but I can still do the things I need to do to be successful.

"I want people to understand that there's more to me than just athleticism. That's not my whole game. Obviously, it's allowed me to do some great things out on the floor. But my basketball IQ and the way I approach the game mentally, I want that to be seen more than my athleticism."

LeBron just passed forty-one thousand minutes played at a younger age than anyone in league history. He's averaging twenty-six points, eight assists, and five rebounds a game, playing too many minutes, and clearly resting himself ON the court. As are many of his teammates, night in and night out, especially on defense.

After Blatt's apology, the Cavs peel off three wins in a row, then fly to Miami for a Christmas Day game, where they get waxed by the Heat. LeBron gets booed each time he touches the ball, and misses eight free throws. Love is starting at center because Varejão, who has missed 165 games over the past four seasons, now has a torn Achilles and will be gone for the balance of the season. Kevin Love, who doesn't relish physical contact, avoids any, committing zero personal fouls in thirty-nine minutes and looking for all the world as if he'd rather be starring for the T-Wolves.

LeBron played another forty minutes on Christmas, and the next night, against Orlando, he looks sluggish on both sides of the ball, and Kyrie's out with a sore knee, and midway through the third quarter it looks like the Cavs are on their way to another L, when the Magic's Tobias Harris swings an elbow too close and gets into it with LeBron, the two of them jawing nose to nose before teammates pull them away, which is to only say that the next physical altercation LeBron James gets into on the court will be his first—and it won't be against this twenty-two-year-old fool on a crap team on the day after Christmas.

Instead, LeBron roasts Harris for fifteen fourth-quarter

points. Guarded by LeBron, Harris scores one. The Cavs win by nine.

"It wasn't the elbow, it was the words he said that got me going," James says. "I was actually in chill mode tonight, but chill mode was deactivated after that."

Chill mode. That's some dry-aged red meat there, brother. The Blatt fans are going to love that one. Chill mode. I can't wait to try it out on an editor.

JAMES HAS A LOT of Bronsplaining to do—not just chill mode ("It was the second game of a back-to-back and I was just feeling the game out like I always do. It had nothing to do with me not playing hard.")—but also the revealed audio accompanying his Christmas postgame hug with his compadre Wade, during which, muffled by on-court noise, it sounds like LeBron's telling Wade, "If things aren't better this year, we're gonna reunite again and do some bigger and better things, all right?"

Be still my heart. Say it ain't so, Bron.

"I've seen the clip just like you've seen the clip," LeBron says. "I don't know exactly what I said at the beginning, either. I know I said, 'We'll get back together and do some bigger and better things,' but it had nothing to do about basketball. I mean, if I was going to tell him that, I'd tell him the night before. Come on—I'm not stupid. I know I didn't go to college but I'm not stupid."

So you're going back to Miami?

"I'm here to build something great in the present and the future, and that's the reason I'm back. I've got no other reason to have to continue to talk about things that're so outlandish. I'm here, this is where I'll be, and this is where I'm comfortable."

I wish someone would tell his face; he looks drawn, haggard, beat. He's aging like a president in office, a month per week. I don't believe for a second that he's leaving the Cavs again, mind you. It's not a matter of faith or trust; it's simple, obvious: LeBron can't walk back his homecoming, can't uproot his wife and children and turn his back on Cleveland again, can't turn the greatest shoe commercial in history into a lie. Twelve NBA seasons and two championships deep into his career, he'd lose all credibility as a human being, and forever taint his basketball legacy.

On the other side of the ledger stands the truth, also simple and obvious: If LeBron leads the Cavs to the first Cleveland sports championship in half a century, if he can roll away that stone, his will be the greatest story ever told. Ever. In human history. ALL of it, including the Big Bang

WHICH LEAVES DAVID BLATT, David *Blatt*, DAVID *BLATT.* Had LeBron as much clout as everyone thinks, Blatt might not make it through New Year's Eve. In the Cavs' next game, Sunday night at home against a Detroit Pistons team boasting six wins and twenty-three losses, they get their asses kicked, 103-90.

The season is a third gone, and their want of effort has come to define them. Tonight they score thirty-three points in the entire second half. Kyrie's still out with a bruised knee—Irving has tended to bruise, or worse, since his single season at Duke, most of which he sat, injured; Blatt is riding him for more than forty minutes a night—and LeBron looks unwell and uninterested, missing fourteen of his nineteen shots, committing seven turnovers, and yet coming within three assists of a triple-double, because LeBron James at his worst is still the best player on the court.

As often happens, the Cavs jump out to a lead, play shabby defense, give back the lead, and call it a night. In thirty games, they are 18-12, fifteen of those wins coming in streaks. Miami was 21-9 after LeBron's first thirty games there. But the Heat played tougher defense, played meaner overall. In their last ten games, the Cavs are 5-5. Their defense is among the NBA's worst by the numbers, and it is painful to watch. In their signature losses—to the Hawks by twenty-nine, and tonight's—they have given up. They simply quit playing hard enough to win.

After the Sunday-night debacle against Detroit, Blatt is asked directly for the first time if he's worried that he's lost control of the team.

"I'm not concerned about that at all," he says. "I'm more concerned about how we're playing."

But the media, they are deeply concerned—deeply, deeply. They have sources. They have heard whispers. Their questions are based on their expectation that Blatt is a dead Jew walking.

After Blatt, who meets the media postgame in a tunnel close to the locker room, the scrum re-forms around LeBron's double-wide locker, and someone asks if a loss like this is a learning experience.

"A loss is a loss, man."

Could it be a learning experience for a rookie head coach? LeBron scowls.

"That's not an answer for me, man. Don't try that."

At practice the next day, they're voicing their deep concern to David Blatt about whether his team truly respects and listens to him.

Blatt assures them that, yes, the Cavs truly do.

"We didn't win eighteen games without there being respect or understanding or attentiveness or any of those things. When things go a little bit bad, some people want to pin those questions because they seem to be the easy thing to do. I think that's unfair and really not to the point.

"We lost a couple games, and last night did not look good, and we did not respond well to it during the game. I recognize that. And certainly when that happens, I'm every bit as much a part of that as everybody else—but it has nothing to do with questions along the lines of what I've heard. I just don't think that's right or fair. I really don't."

Fair? Pouting is a bad look for a dude making $3 million a year, wearing his Sunday-best gray suit and silver tie. Fair is a hard sell in the face of such deep concern.

After practice, someone asks LeBron straight up: Is David Blatt the right coach for the Cavs?

"Yeah, he's our coach, I mean, what other coach do we have?"

Jelly donuts! Bear claws! Come on, LeBron, wouldn't your head coach look better and feel more secure if you'd offer him a more heartfelt endorsement than that?

"Listen man, I don't pay no bills around here. Man, I play. He's our coach. To make it a feud between me and Blatt or the team and Blatt, it's just to sell—to get people to read it and put something at the bottom of the ticker. That's all it is."

Not all. The media is the media is the media—I may work in a higher-end brothel, but we're all in the same business. My journo nephews aren't ginning up this stuff; they're just working the stories in front of them—LeBron's minutes, LeBron's aging body, LeBron's slumped body language, LeBron running LeBron's offense, LeBron ignoring or literally boxing out Blatt during time-outs so LeBron can freely rant at miscreant teammates.

The media say less than they know. Dan Gilbert's trigger finger's twitching. LeBron's people want Blatt fired and replaced by Mark Jackson, who was fired in June by Golden State after the Warriors lost in the first round of the playoffs. Jackson, a loud evangelical Christian and a lousy head coach, signed with LeBron's agent two weeks after The Homecoming.

I pity David Blatt, but with more than fifty games to go and his job at risk, I'm more fearful than ever that Blatt will push his key players too hard, particularly LeBron, but Kyrie, too. Even Kevin Love now prances stiffly back up the court on D—not that he was quick before—wincing like a fellow whose lower back refuses to unclench, waving his pale arms as the man he's guarding darts past him to the rim.

I'm also starting to fret about the NBA's other Big Story, Golden State. Playing for a rookie coach themselves—erstwhile Cleveland Cavalier Steve Kerr—the Warriors blast out 21-2 in the much tougher Western Conference. Now Pip and I will have to stay up late to scout West Coast games, but this much I already know: Steve Kerr would not be running this version of LeBron James out there for forty minutes a game, or let himself get boxed out from a sideline huddle.

Something has to give—someone has to go—and soon.

11

ROSH HASHANAH

LeBron turns thirty on December 30, two days after the Pistons loss. CNBC wishes him a happy birthday at 5:47 a.m., as the dog and I scout the Asian and European markets, and notes that he'll rake in $53 million from his endorsement deals this year.

He sits out the game that night against the Hawks with a left knee injury.

"It's been hurting pretty much all year," he says. "I've been playing with it, and it goes away and comes back."

Uh-oh.

"All the tests and everything I've done with the doctors—everything has come back negative. So I'm not concerned. I've got forty-one thousand minutes in my career including the playoffs. *You* drive that car in the wintertime."

He says he expects to be ready for the next game.

Without LeBron, the Cavs lose to the Hawks, 109-101. Love leaves the game in the third quarter with back spasms and watches the rest of the game in the locker room with

LeBron. Kyrie goes off for thirty-five points, but also commits eight turnovers. They now sit five full games behind Atlanta, with four other teams between.

None of this seems to faze David Blatt.

"I thought we came out and competed. You saw a team that was together and fighting, after some good-hearted soul-searching and talking and teammanship, leadership from within—and the kind of grit we should have as Cleveland people."

Look at the shit-eating grin on this *vantz*. His team loses for the third time in four games and he's praising them for competing, bragging about Cleveland grit, and gushing about Kyrie, back from his injury.

"He's just a wonderful, wonderful young man," Blatt says. "I just think the world of that kid—he understands what this is about and is doing everything he can to impact us in a positive way. I just thought Kyrie played his heart out—I can't say enough about that kid."

Maybe he's just trying to rally his troops—Love's hurt, Varejão's done for the year, the Cavs are 0-3 so far when LeBron sits, Shawn Marion sprained his ankle—but Blatt's paean to Kyrie is, in its specifics and its effusion, an arrow aimed dead at LeBron.

Whatever prompts his eruption, Blatt sounds nothing like a coach concerned about his job. Dan Gilbert, with David Griffin in his ear, isn't going to pull the trigger. David Blatt is going nowhere.

Of course. Only Cleveland would hire a coach with no

NBA experience, a Jew to boot, hand him a hammer and nails, and let him revise the New Testament.

ON ME SAINTED MOTHER'S head, LeBron visits me in a dream that very night. I'm serious. We're sitting in an office somewhere, no place I know, wearing suits, talking. I feel guilty, ashamed, but I've already said whatever it was I had to say, and I can't recall a word.

LeBron's quiet, looking straight ahead. His hands are clasped beneath his chin, elbows on his knees. His brow is furrowed.

I rise to take my leave.

"Stop worrying, man," LeBron says. His voice is deep and not unkind. "I got this."

Cool.

"Good to see you've been taking care of yourself."

Thanks, man. Good luck.

That's all I can remember. I ascribe no meaning to it beyond its face: I am insane. Lost in the fun house, deep in the weeds.

HAPPY NEW YEAR. LeBron returns Blatt's fuck-you with his own: Bye-bye. He's taking two weeks off, to get right. Sore knee. Sore back. Strained spirit. Sprained ass. He takes off for Miami, just like that. The Cavs' statement says he's expected back in two weeks.

Two weeks. Six games.

Miami? Nothing in there about Miami.

WE RING IN 2015 in the usual way, with a rib roast and sparkling cider and midnight ice cream sodas. Norman Rockwell on Easter in Mayberry couldn't paint a sweeter scene. Fireplace. Dog. Two toilets.

I'm miserable. Up all night on BasketballReference.com, streaming replays, and sulking.

My third-floor office, half an attic, with a plastic hospital piss jug for a toilet, feels like my grandfather's basement cell.

Two more weeks and the season's half-gone. That's reality.

Also: This is no championship team. I have no story to tell here beyond an athlete getting old and a city doomed to lose forever and an elderly Jew with back hair dreaming about a tender young athlete.

Indeed, I have no weapon.

Therefore, I require a plan.

Miami? Maybe I'll run into the King.

Nah. I have doctor's appointments. I'll survive—this ain't *Tuesdays with LeBron*—but I have the urologist, ophthalmologist, and my annual physical. Also a shingles shot.

Besides, LeBron is not the problem.

David Blatt is not the problem.

I am the problem. I'm writing a book, not a dream journal. It's time to make my move. The Cavs are in Philly Monday night—I know I can get a credential. I'll write David Blatt a letter and have it ready to give him after the game. If my luck stays good, I can maybe ask him, Jew to Jew, to put in a good word for Judah at his alma mater.

> *Dear Coach Blatt,*
>   My name is Scott Raab and I'm writing a book about the Cavaliers and the city of Cleveland. This will be more or less a sequel to my 2011 book, *The Whore of Akron,* based mainly on the Cavs and Cleveland during the 2009–2011 seasons.
>   One of that book's two epigraphs is a Malamud quote ["All men are Jews . . ."] cited early in your Princeton thesis. I'm no Malamud and no sportswriter, either; I've been at *Esquire* magazine since 1997. The Cavaliers credentialed me for the 2009–10 and 2010–11 seasons, but Tad Carper has denied me access, even for Media Day in September. He gave me no reason for denying my application, and while I have no wish to complicate his job or yours, I'd very much enjoy meeting you. No quotes, no columns, no headlines.
> *Best,*

I know the Tad Carper bit is dicey, but finessing the fact that I'm persona non grata would be foolish; better David Blatt should hear it from me first, wrapped in an appeal to our literary kinship. I must be the only soul alive not named

David Blatt who ever read his thesis—and trust me: he chose the right line of work.

The day before the Cavs arrive in Philly, they play Dallas in Cleveland, and David Griffin tells the media before the game to stop telling tales of David Blatt's job security.

"This narrative of our coaching situation is truly ridiculous," Griffin says. "It's a non-story. It's a non-narrative. Coach Blatt is our coach. He's going to remain our coach. That narrative is done. No change is being made. Period."

Griffin, who started his NBA life as a media relations intern with the Suns when he was still an Arizona State political science major in the early '90s, doesn't just supply punctuation: He revises, too.

"Do not write that as a vote of confidence—he never needed one. It was never a question. So don't write it that way."

See, this is why I told my kid he could be anything he wanted in this world except an editor. Shape your own narrative, tell your own truth in this world, instead of parroting some barely-forty goateed ginger who prattles like an HR rep.

"We have a chance to galvanize ourselves and grow and move in a positive direction, so I just want to make sure we're doing that in a fresh environment."

Thus galvanized, the doughty Cavs go hard for the entire first quarter. The Mavericks, unimpeded by anything resembling defense, shoot 56 percent and win by nineteen.

Worse, Kyrie's back seizes up and he leaves the game early in the second half.

"This sucks," Kyrie tells the press after the game.

Yep.

IT'S COLD IN PHILLY, bitter cold. The Sixers are 4-28 and they've lost all fourteen of their home games so far this season, but the place is packed with fans who bought tickets months ago, in anticipation of seeing LeBron demolish their team.

Dion's due to start with Kyrie out, and has left fifty tickets for friends and family to come watch him torch the Wells Fargo Center, but he never returns to the floor after warm-ups. Nor do Alex Kirk and Lou Amundson, two tall white bookends David Blatt shelves on the bench.

There must be a trade. I don't know what it is, but someone bit on Dion, or Griffin decided to sell cheap just to move him out.

Blatt trots out a starting lineup I haven't seen the like of since early in the 1960s: four cloddish white guys and Tristan Thompson. Love racks up one of his old Timberwolves stat lines—twenty-eight points, nineteen rebounds—but no one on the Cavs wants to play defense in the fourth quarter, and Cleveland blows a seventeen-point lead and loses, 95-92, to the worst team in the league, a team that's bad *on purpose,* a team whose strategy, freely admitted, is to lose as many games as possible and own the draft.

The Philly fans loved every second.

I find out at halftime that Dion was yanked from the lineup ninety seconds before tip-off because David Griffin, whom I could possibly learn to love, in time, sprinkled pixie dust, turning Dion into J. R. Smith and Iman Shumpert, plus a first-round draft pick.

It is more than a trade: it is a miracle.

It is also awkward, mediawise. A shaky team, a ridiculous loss, a blockbuster trade—the mood downstairs is somber, even hushed, after the defeat. Blatt mutters a few minutes of clichés to the pack of reporters and ducks back through the door.

I'm waiting for him to come back out, in the hallway, my letter in hand, when I'm joined by a nice young Jewish couple. The woman is Israeli—Blatt coached her—and she's excited to see him again.

Blatt lights up the moment he opens the door and spots her. Big hug, and they're going a mile a minute in Hebrew, which is Greek to me. I'm standing by, gaping, my flimsy single-game credential dangling from a white elastic string around my neck.

Blatt glances sideways at me and stops talking.

"Who are you?"

Scott Raab. I'm writing a book. I brought a letter.

Those may be the three dumbest sentences I've ever spoken in sequence, but a plan's a plan. I hand Blatt the envelope and he takes it, folds it, stuffs it in his inside jacket pocket, and resumes speaking *Ivrit* to the woman.

TWO WEEKS TURNS OUT to be just right for all concerned. Two days after flipping Kobe Wade, David Griffin, the greatest basketball mind since Red Auerbach ran the Celtics, turns a pair of first-round draft picks—including the one he stole for Dion—into Timofey Pavlovich Mozgov, a mountain standing seven feet one inch tall and 275 pounds wide. Hailing from Saint Petersburg, he played for David Blatt when Blatt coached the Russian national team to the bronze in the 2012 Olympics. He's not nimble and can't jump, but he runs the court just fine for his mass, and he'll play defense at the rim. Above all, he'll try hard, if only because he considers Blatt a legitimate head coach.

David Griffin, hardwood Einstein, is kvelling. As he should be.

"His numbers didn't need to be flashy. We've got three guys that are top-twenty players in the NBA—those guys can be flashy. We need guys that do the dirty work."

Guys, plural. Shumpert has a shoulder that needs a couple of weeks to heal, but he's a tall, quick young guard who likes to defend. JR, a salary dump for Phil Jackson, comes with his own narrative, the object of amusement and suspicion both, demonized, a scary clown, with back and neck tattoos and tweets suspected for years of being gang-y by people who find such things glamorous at a safe distance.

The truth is that JR is in his tenth NBA season because his three-point range is Mars, and when Griffin asks LeBron about the deal, LeBron, who got to know JR when they were high school stars and NBA phenoms—JR was nineteen when he came into the league straight from high school in LeBron's second NBA season—says yes please to the trade.

He's still a week away from playing, but LeBron flies back from Miami and joins the Cavs for a West Coast road trip. There has been no mention yet, from the team or the media, of his Miami sojourn, and he's careful in his public judgment of Griffin's moves.

"Those are three pieces that can help us, but until we get healthy and get on the floor together, we won't be able to know. Once we see our pieces on the floor, Coach Blatt and the coaching staff will do a great job seeing what lineups, what pieces, work well together."

Cautious, yes. But not entirely devoid of warmth.

Coach Blatt returns the favor by attributing LeBron's absence on the Cavs' bench during games to doctors' orders.

"He's not supposed to be doing a whole lot of continuous sitting," says Blatt. "Do I miss him? Yes. I miss him as a player, a lot, and I miss him as a person being around. I do."

His teammates miss him more. It's not just the points, rebounds, and assists—twenty-five, five, and eight, All-Star averages for any other player in the league—but the shield he provides. As long as he's the headline—and LeBron is always the headline—their own lassitude is a sidebar, if that. Without him on the court, they soil themselves on a nightly basis.

The Cavs open the West Coast trip by losing to the Warriors, who barely break a sweat, by eighteen points; Golden State is 29-5. Then Sacramento, no powerhouse, drubs them by nineteen. This is Cleveland's ninth loss in ten games, their fifth in a row. Their record now is 19-19, sixth-best in the weak Eastern Conference.

LeBron's missing statistics aren't the real culprit here. The Cleveland Cavaliers just don't play hard enough to win, especially on defense. Instead of a Big Three, they have aging LeBron, who has missed more games already this season than in any full season of his career, and two soft young stars, Irving and Love, who've never even played a playoff game, and who seem to worry more about their stats than winning.

On the upside, their rookie head coach knows what it takes to win, in Milan. And, of course, they have whatever's left of LeBron.

WHAT'S LEFT OF HIM is evident four minutes into the first quarter against Phoenix, two days after the Kings loss, when he bolts past two defenders from the baseline and cuts under the rim, turning as he leaps to reverse-slam over the Suns' seven-foot center, Alex Len.

I'm out of the chair, on my feet, hollering YES! My heart is singing. I think that's singing. I take two eighty-one-milligram aspirin, just in case of infarction. Continuous sitting isn't good for anybody.

It's a strange and wonderful loss. LeBron's slashing, slicing, hitting threes. He's rusty, missing free throws, turning the ball over on ridiculous passes, but you can see the speed and bounce and joy back in his game. JR, starting at the two, leads the Cavs back from nineteen down with fifteen points

of his own in the third quarter, but the shabby defense—
Kevin Love, torched by the immortal Markieff Morris, is
benched for the whole fourth quarter—and Kyrie's eight
turnovers are too much for the Cavs to overcome.

The strange occurs early in the second quarter, when
LeBron gets called for an offensive foul and starts jawing at
the ref near the Cavs' bench, and David Blatt, in a not ignoble effort to be a stand-up rookie head coach, attempts to
sidle between James and the official, whereupon LeBron lays
hands on Blatt and shoves him away, back to his seat.

It is unusual to see any NBA player—never mind any NFL
player—manhandle his coach. LeBron bumped shoulders
with Erik Spoelstra on his way back to the bench for a time-
out during his first year in Miami, and it was huge news for
days. Tonight's official line—Blatt and LeBron explain after
the game that James was only trying to save his coach from
a technical foul—doesn't change the media narrative, despite
David Griffin's stirring nonvote of confidence.

None of this means dick to me, quite honestly. I don't
have to file a game story and choose the word—*shove, push,*
or *nudge?*—for what LeBron did to Blatt. I don't care that the
Cavs are now 19-20 or that LeBron finishes with thirty-three
points. I care only that he's back, swagger intact.

He's King James again.

"I couldn't make those moves two weeks ago," LeBron says
after the game. "For me to come back and feel like myself
again is pretty cool."

Yes. Oh, yes. Yes.

"I haven't felt like this in a long time," he says.

Me neither, LeBron. Years. Years and years.

Pathetic, I know, but no less true for that: I missed him. I missed him more than David Blatt or his teammates. I missed the hope of a championship, sure, but it goes beyond that. Some of my love is hero worship, fanboy drool. Some of it's aesthetic; the sheer beauty of athletic performance gets short shrift compared with dance, but I see no reason why it should. And some of it, the best part, is a visceral joy jolting me onto my feet, roaring, strong and free, young once more.

I barely remember myself that way. I *need* LeBron. My own athletic prime was brief, and neither athletic nor prime, but I was young and I was strong, and bestrode the globe like a colossus if I wasn't blacked out. I had no plan, but I had a .22. I didn't waddle or ache then. I walked like a man.

Thanks to Sandy and Jim Brown, I had swag. I'd like to strut some for my son, but now I'm a lump in a maple rocking chair with my laptop on a folding tray and a game on. If he's lucky, like tonight, I'm in fresh sweatpants.

"I don't know why you need a rocking chair," Judah says. "I've never seen you rock."

I'm too tired from making money to rock. Princeton costs.

The kid's 529 account is pretty much all the juice I have left, and Judah knows it and knows I know he knows it. I'm slow up the stairs and on the treadmill. He's fast. He's on his way to strong. After my L7 disk crumbled three years ago, before I bought the treadmill, he walked me up and down the block, my arm and bulk sagging over his shoulders. There are secrets between us, but not the fact that he's fifteen years old and I'm sixty-two.

"My balls itch," Judah says.

I don't believe I've ever heard him say that before. I make a note of it. It makes me proud somehow. He has a set. He'll need 'em, even with a 529. Soon enough, he'll be moving on.

Balls. Swag. Confidence. I sold and bartered years of mine, piece by piece at a decent price, and time's taking the rest. What's left is this: Writing. Pondering LeBron.

Soon enough, King James, too, will move on. Not yet. *Please* not yet. Part of me is lost without LeBron. I found it tonight. Again.

IT'S STILL A CLEVELAND team. In Los Angeles the next day, Blatt's denying a report that Ty Lue, not Blatt, is calling Cavs time-outs, that Love is unhappy being pulled, that elders Miller, Marion, and Jones hold Blatt in contempt and disparage him freely, that Kyrie and LeBron ignore his play-calling.

All of this is true, and none of it matters, because King James is back. It is no dream; the whole team is awake. Against the Lakers, Love takes a charge late in the game, bad back be damned—he just plants himself in the lane, with a ten-point lead, knowing that Jeremy Lin will jump into him, and holds his ground, toppling backward, slow and stiff, drawing the foul. Love stays down, laughing, and three Cavs, LeBron included, come to help him off the floor.

Love standing tough and giving up his body means far

more than the win itself—the Lakers with Kobe on his last legs are nearly as hopeless as the Sixers—more than the end of the losing streak, more than LeBron's thirty-six points. Postgame, LeBron says so.

"What Kevin did tonight, playing through the injuries, he just toughed it out. He battled on the glass. Even with his back, feeling like he couldn't keep playing, he took a charge. There are moments in the season where you know your team is taking a step forward—to have one of your big guys do that is huge."

YES! The Cavs' win against the Lakers kicks off a twelve-game winning streak—three solid weeks of swagger and bliss. LeBron's bearing down every game, running the floor and the offense; Irving and Love sweat on D; fortified by Mozgov at the rim, the Cavs hold ten consecutive foes under a hundred points, winning all ten games.

The only sour note is David Blatt. Even after the Cavs return, pounding the Bulls at the Q—Mozgov, who has excellent footwork for a golem, decent hands, and a nice shooting touch, dominates Pau Gasol—Blatt's Euroego stays firmly stuck in his craw.

"We wanted to come home and show that we had actually moved from one point to the next in a positive direction. Despite all the crap that has been said and written, a lot of it unfair and a lot of it ugly, we stayed the course."

Please, my kike. Give me a call, shoot me an e-mail. Pronto. You'd better serve yourself and the Cavs if you'd just humble down and shut the fuck up. Here's what happened:

You got back the best basketball player who ever lived, and he has laid down the law, and his teammates are paying close attention now. Your players know it. So does every member of the sports media in America. Stop whining and enjoy the ride. LeBron's home for real and everything is possible again.

ALMOST EVERYTHING: BLATT DOESN'T CALL. He just changed agents a few weeks ago, so I leave a message for his new agent. Nada.

I'm dug in at the Liberty Bell, alone. I go to games alone. It's the dead of winter, the playoffs are months away, but I have to see this team for myself.

The Cavaliers are marvelous to behold. Against Charlotte, they score seventy-five points IN THE FIRST HALF, and—mirabile dictu—confine the Hornets to forty. It is nearly perfect basketball. JR is on fire. Shumpert is electric in his first ten minutes as a Cav, a dervish with a Devils Tower of hair. Mozgov's strong and confident, and his footwork and mobility are a delight. Kyrie is pure silk. Love looks lost in the offensive barrage, but looks better on defense. He's trying.

Above all, there is LeBron. With my own eyes I see the real King James out there again: In twenty-seven minutes, he puts up twenty-five points, nine assists, six rebounds, and four steals. He's a maestro, a freak, a gift, a small forward, a power forward, *and* a point guard, doing it all while coaching the team.

Charlotte's no great shakes, but they've won eight of their

last nine. At one point, the Cavs go up by forty-nine. I'm on my feet half the game, hugging the woman seated next to me and high-fiving her husband. We made friends before the game—if I'm not sitting with the media, I feel weird in the crowd at a Cleveland game, scribbling in my tiny notebook.

This is my town, my team. These are my people. I don't want to feel alone.

The hugging, though—it lasts too long, and it involves too much body. Unless it's my imagination.

Nope.

Jimbo—not his real name—got the seats through the place he works, and he and Linda—not her real name, either—are happy as hell. Why not? It's Friday night, the beer is cold, and the Cavs are freaking awesome. I haven't had a beer since 1994, but I'm happy to be with them, laughing and cheering.

Linda's been handsy. Nothing flagrant—my arm, my shoulder, my knee. Now the hugging.

Everyone stays until the final horn. It's Cleveland.

While we wait for our row to get moving, Jimbo mentions that he and Linda swing, and if I'm into it, there's a party.

I'm honored and I say so, but I must demur.

I've never played anything but one-on-one, but I truly am honored. I peg them for their midforties, and nothing special to look at, but neither am I. It's always nice to be desired.

It's also better for me to be faithful. For ME, I say. Others may compartmentalize or swing; I can't. My sainted mother went through three husbands; Sandy plundered two marriages; I'm already with my second wife. I may not know what love is, but I know damn well what Sandy Raab would do.

Besides, I have pretzel rods and mustard at the condo, and—thanks to technological miracles that occurred after I turned forty, and which amaze me beyond belief; I used to go to the public library to research stories—I now carry a device that delivers moving images even more enticing than Jimbo's and Linda's, and it fits into my other hand should I care to crank it up.

It also streams the postgame interviews.

"Right now, I feel like this is the team that I envisioned," LeBron's saying.

Yes.

"How we share the ball."

Yes, LeBron. Yes.

"How we defend."

Oh, yes.

"This is the style of basketball I envisioned."

God *damn* it. Yes. Yesyesyesyes.

"Let's not get ahead of ourselves," says Blatt. "We've got a long way to go."

Understood. You in particular, sheeny cockblock.

But I can tell Blatt's thinking what I know LeBron's thinking:

The Cavs are good enough to win it all. Yes.

12

A LONG, LONG WAY TO GO

Did somebody say maestro? LeBron doesn't just make David Blatt a better basketball coach and his teammates better players; I'm *killing* this shit. Three straight *Esquire* covers. That's me, sitting courtside with Will Smith at a Sixers game, up on the Jumbotron. I'm at yoga class with Charlize Theron. This old yid's still flying first class.

None of it is writing, exactly, not even the writing. Thirty years of magazine work, thirty years on the road. Never won a prize, but I always do my best, even on the celebrity profiles. I'm nothing if not an honest craftsman. It's not art; it's my job. A word count. A deadline. A business.

The business has changed, and the business is vital to me. In 1998, Granger needs a column for the front of the magazine; for the next eleven years, I'm Answer Fella every month. But now—now the *Esquire* website needs a thousand deeply felt words of reminiscence and tribute on the passing of Lou Reed or Philip Seymour Hoffman or David Carr, and

I am at a loss for the first time in my writing life, too stunned and sad to type crap about them and their fate.

I need time, and every day there's less of it ahead, less time and more sadness. I can put it into words—I can't NOT put it into words—but I'm not a gumball machine. I write slow. I'm old, and I feel more, and I feel more deeply. That's how it's supposed to be.

LeBron needs fewer minutes. I need more. I look at my son and see him at every age all at once, and know he's bound for elsewhere, without me. I see my wife smile, and I don't ever want to hit the road again, not without her.

I see LeBron play, I watch the Cavs win, and I am happy, happy in the moment and the promise of glory.

"When you're a true professional, and true to the game, the game gives back to you," he says one night at his locker. "Always."

He's right. I found out at the famous and prestigious Iowa Writers' Workshop (Motto: ALWAYS LET 'EM KNOW YOU WENT TO THE WORKSHOP) that unless you are a poet or a teacher, writing is business. Agents and editors would come, scouting for ripe talent—and the talent would step on each other to get close.

I was thirty-two already and drinking hard, but I paid close attention, pushed every break as hard and far as I could, and tried to stay true to the craft.

Enough is enough.

If I can hang on to the *Esquire* job for two more years and see Judah off to college, I'll take early retirement—no awards, but I'm the last magazine hack in America with a pension—and then maybe Lisa and I can call our own next shot.

Cleveland? I will buff away the patina of its misery. I'll mentor youth and see if anything comes out of me without a word count or a deadline. Lisa can have me planted in Lake View Cemetery, near Ray Chapman's section.

Or Ireland. I'll recollect, in tranquility—just me, a bottomless pint, and Lisa's vegan chili—and write poetry. After I pass by, she'll toss my ashes to the wind in County Sligo.

Either way, I figure ten or fifteen years, if that, of relative puissance and clarity, followed by oblivion eternal.

It's not a weapon or a plan. It's fate's best case.

Trust me on this: If you do get to your sixties, don't let anything come between you and your existential dread. Love hard, but never forget that we die alone under a pitiless sun. If you're not feeling existential dread in your sixties, pally, you're not really living.

THE BEST PART OF winning like the Cavs are winning now is that you can see Kyrie and LeBron fusing. After Kyrie sinks a dagger three in a revenge win against the Pistons, LeBron grabs Irving on the court and pulls him close, chest to chest—LeBron lit by some warrior lust and streaming sweat, Kyrie deadpan, sloe-eyed.

LeBron needs this part of it, the brotherhood, has craved

and created it all his life on the basketball court. Dwyane Wade was a big brother in Miami, a friend who entered the league the same year, and an NBA champion himself; Kyrie might be one or two generations of hoops younger, but he's no one's kid brother. He's a Dukie, arrogant, with the game of an ancient wizard, and the Cavaliers have coddled him just as they once did LeBron.

LeBron barks something at him in that hug, and Kyrie, lighting up, breaks his smile wide open.

After the game, when someone asks him what LeBron said, Kyrie stays true to the game.

"I think the moment's still out there on the floor, and I think that's where it's gonna stay."

Nice. Perfect.

Kyrie just torched Detroit for thirty-eight. Next game, with LeBron out with a sore wrist, he goes for fifty-five—the league high so far this season, one point shy of LeBron's franchise record—to beat the Blazers.

Like warm spring rain, the wins come. The 44-10 Warriors come to play at the Q, and JR and Shumpert defend Curry and Klay Thompson hard, Mozgov outbigs Andrew Bogut, and LeBron, all too aware that he has already been written off for this year's MVP due to Steph Curry's historically great three-point shooting and pouting beauty, explodes for forty-two—Curry and Thompson combined get thirty-one—and Cleveland kicks their golden ass.

The Cavs stood at 19-20 when LeBron returned; now

they're 37-22. And David Blatt keeps blatting. LeBron's running the offense; LeBron takes himself out of games when he feels the need; LeBron's getting the credit for the Cavs' turnaround. Blatt, with all the media titans in town for the Golden State game, sets them straight.

"I've been a head coach for twenty-two years. People overlook that too easily. I know that I'm the new kid on the block in the NBA, and I recognize the greatness of this league and the difficulty of this league—and the fact that I still am going through the adjustments I have to make to coach in this league—but I am not now, nor was I, nor have I been for quite some time, a rookie coach."

It is as elegant an expression of seething resentment as I've ever heard from an NBA coach, and further evidence, as if any were needed, of Princeton's standards. The media are sympathetic to the difficulty of Blatt's position, and thousands of columns have already been written blaming LeBron's detachment and disrespect for Blatt's rocky road, but he sounds petty, not pleased, and more than slightly ridiculous in the flush of his team's success.

In truth, Blatt's done a decent job, and that should be enough. Because of or despite him, the Cavs are playing better defense, and if they're not sharing the ball according to the EuroPrinceton way, it may be because they start every game with two ball-dominant stars, one of them the best basketball player heaven and hard work ever made. Blatt can take full credit for not standing in their way, and for not calling me to spill his soul.

LEBRON'S RUNNING HOT EVERYWHERE—on the court, on Twitter, on Instagram. He's the players' union's new executive vice president. He is a mogul: an investor, a Hollywood producer, an entrepreneur, half of a billionaire. I sold him way short, him and Rich Paul and Maverick Carter, guys he grew up with, his partners to this day. Worse, I sold them short with a contempt that now feels, I must say, racist at its core.

How smart could a bunch of Akron black guys be? I mean, it's one thing to feel all the outrage an elderly Jew can feel about police shootings and systemic racism in America, but seriously: How smart can a bunch of Akron black guys be?

I laughed when Carter used the phrase "global icon" ten years ago, after LeBron fired his agent. They had a plan to build his career into an empire—Bron and Mav and Richie and Randy Mims, LeBron's cousin. The Four Horsemen. What a joke.

In *The Whore of Akron*, I referred to them all as "the Akron chapter of Mensa," if memory serves, which I assure you it does.

"I think I've grown as an individual and a businessman," LeBron said then. "The opportunities I have in front of me, in order for us to make that happen, I wanted to pull the train."

LeBron James is barely thirty now, and he is a global icon. And Maverick Carter is an occasional guest lecturer at Harvard.

I have a fully vested pension. And, of course, two toilets.

ALONG WITH THE WINS come the narratives. The one I have to be careful with is spelled HGH. There are whispers and rumors, not only among my nephews, but reaching up to the kingdom of Bill Simmons—he and the estimable Zach Lowe have a clammy podcast exchange alluding to the subject— that part of LeBron's recuperation in Miami included chemical enhancement.

The speculation isn't new, but it has never gone mainstream. It isn't my intent to make it so, and I have nothing to add as a reporter, but I'd strongly prefer NOT to avoid it, mainly because LeBron James has been the NBA's best overall player since his second season, when he was twenty years old and averaged twenty-seven points, with seven rebounds and seven assists per game—and somehow, even after all the minutes, seasons, and years, he remains so.

Over the last five seasons alone, he has played twenty-five hundred more minutes than any other player in the league, and his ability to avoid serious injury is nothing short of freakish. Whatever he did while rehabbing in Miami worked wonders.

No one knows. No one really wants to know. The league and the media are business partners. It's a fun thing to hint at and josh about, and that's all. When the league announced in April that it would begin testing its players' blood for violations of NBA drug policy, LeBron seems sanguine.

"If it's the rules, it's the rules," he says. "It shouldn't be a problem."

Good enough for me. I don't know, and I don't care. There is a profound issue here—several, really, that boil down to one:

Who owns LeBron James? Dan Gilbert and I may have thought we did, but we were wrong. LeBron owns LeBron. We have come to terms with that, Dan and I.

Let me put it another way. When I was courtside with Will Smith, many of the young players came over to pay respect—to him, not to me. They aren't much older than Judah, and while they've already succeeded wildly, most of them won't make it, and for the few who do, the average NBA career lasts about five seasons, with average earnings totaling $25 million.

Will Smith got $28 million for *I, Robot* alone and routinely pulls down twenty. He risks nothing on a shoot but his reputation, and his career will endure as long as he can walk and talk. He won't get cut or traded to Salt Lake City. If he moves, no furious asshat will write a book about it.

And nobody will ever ask Will Smith to piss into a cup to prove he's clean.

Is that because it's only show business, so unlike pro sports, the purest, fairest, finest expression of humanity?

I think not.

My kid was disappointed when he found out that everyone else knew Barry Bonds used steroids. That's how it goes, I told him. If it's true, it isn't right. Cheating isn't right, hurting your body isn't right.

I don't tell Judah that if I believed that a drug would make me better at my job, I would do it, or that I have.

When he's a grown man, *kinehora*, he'll make his own decisions, just like me. Nobody owns me; nobody owns anyone. My wife and kid are not the sum of my projections, nor is the dog, nor is Will Smith.

Nor is LeBron. He's just a man whose job is to play a hero on the court and save a city in his spare time. He said so himself, and if tragedy needs hubris, fuck tragedy. We're talking playoffs here, not Sophocles.

THEY CLINCH ON MARCH 20 with their fifteenth straight road win. Lisa makes mapo tofu, with ground pork. It's a special night, the Cavs' first playoff berth in five long seasons.

After the game, Kevin Love, who is finally going to taste the postseason, looks miserable, as ever. Staring at the floor, he speaks in a low monotone.

"It feels good," he says.

Back in February, LeBron had tweeted, "Stop trying to find a way to FIT-OUT and just FIT-IN. Be a part of something special! Just my thoughts," which was a message to Love and a bizarre way to call out a teammate. In tonight's second quarter, Love barely moved to contest a layup, and LeBron, screaming, raised his own arms high, as if to demonstrate a fundamental concept of defense to a child.

There are two issues here: Love's defensive fugue states—Blatt has taken to sitting him in the fourth quarter of close games—and Love's grudging surrender to being the third wheel of the Cavs' offense.

"I think it's one of the toughest situations I've had to deal with," Love says. "There's no blueprint for what I should be doing."

Sure there is. It's just much harder and less glamorous than being the only star on a thirty-win team. I don't know what the fit bullshit is about, but I do know that Love has been through his own version of The Decision. His father, Stan, was a University of Oregon legend who went on to a short NBA career; after Kevin, like LeBron a national star in high school, chose UCLA instead, the tsunami of shit that followed included death threats.

I don't know what LeBron knows of this, but I myself get angry with Kevin Love when he plays soft on D. His overall numbers—and the team's numbers with Love in the lineup—are good. They're just not as good as they were on the Timberwolves, and LeBron's giving him shit, and he's twenty-six years old with a new endorsement deal pimping chocolate milk, and he's going to have to step up.

They're all gonna have to step up. Blatt, too. I'm not worried about the Eastern Conference—only the Hawks finish with a better record, and the Cavs are by far the better team. But Golden State—my God. They're not just one of the very best NBA teams I've seen in fifty years of watching, they're also something different, a meld of uncanny shooting talent and the math of 3>2. On a good night, their game flows like Barcelona soccer—and they rarely have a bad night.

ALL CLEVELAND PLAYOFF RUNS are doomed. Their rarity only amplifies the litany of losses past; the knot in my stomach isn't hope. No lead is big enough to feel safe; no mistake is too small to bankrupt hope.

"Nothing is promised," LeBron is fond of saying, and who am I to disagree? Nothing is exactly what is promised.

It's a goddamned nightmare this time around, a killing floor. The Cavs finish the season strong—53-29 for the season—and come into the first round, against the Celtics, healthy and peaking. Kyrie hits for thirty in his first-ever playoff game, with five threes; Love is working hard, fitting in on both ends of the floor; LeBron's superb, with a triple-double in a Game 3 win in Boston—"I love road games in the playoffs," he says at the morning shootaround—to go with Love's twenty-three points and nine rebounds, and some crucial three-point sniping by JR.

The Celtics are game but overmatched. They foul often and, often, with prejudice—chippy, not quite dirty, until, early in Game 4, when, on the cusp of getting swept on their home court, Kelly Olynyk, Boston's backup seven-foot ficus, locks Kevin Love's left arm and, wrenching downward, torques it as he turns Love toward the floor.

It's a filthy fucking play, and Love, cradling his limp left arm, sprints off the court, dashing up the tunnel and into the Cavs' locker room.

We're sitting in the living room, gaping at the TV.

Jesus. That was *ghastly.* Love looked terrified.

"No way he's coming back," Judah says. "That's the fastest I've seen him run all season."

The game gets nastier from there. With Cleveland way ahead, Blatt inserts the venerable Kendrick Perkins late in the first half. Perk is a legend in his own right, a low-post tough guy, the Celts' starting center in 2008, when he was twenty-three. Even then, his game did not involve much running, jumping, or shooting; now he's strictly an enforcer. David Griffin signed him at the end of February for playoff moments just like this, when a punk-ass bitch like Kelly Olynyk takes liberties with a Cavalier.

Olynyk's in asylum on the Boston bench, so Perk comes up on Celtics' forward Jae Crowder, sets a blind pick, and rams Crowder in the chest and neck with both forearms. Crowder comes back at him, ready to tussle, and as the two are separated, Perkins tosses a soft right jab to Crowder's face and draws a Flagrant 1.

After halftime, after the Cavs watch Olynyk's thuggery replayed on video, JR comes out and, with barely a minute gone in the third quarter, starts banging for position with Crowder near the basket as a Boston shot goes up. Slinging a hard right backward, fist balled, Smith clocks Crowder on the jaw. Crowder crumples, writhing, holding his left knee. Two teammates and the trainer walk him to the locker room. JR is ejected for a Flagrant 2, which means he'll also be suspended for at least one game.

The Cavs win, of course, because I need to explain to

Judah that King Pyrrhus actually won two separate battles that together cost him sufficient casualties to make defeat by the fucking Romans inevitable, hence—2,295 years later—the Pyrrhic victory.

The kid doesn't look up. He's got the Rubik's Cube going, timing himself. Love's on the TV, postgame. His arm's in a sling. They reset his dislocated shoulder in the locker room, and no doubt gave him something for the pain besides chocolate milk, because he isn't looking down at the floor or mumbling now. He's pissed off.

"I thought it was a bush-league play," Love says. "Olynyk had no chance to get the ball, and it's just too bad that he would go to those lengths to take somebody out of the game. I have no doubt in my mind that he did that on purpose."

Early word is that he'll miss the next two weeks, minimum. I take consolation in the fact that the kid's down to one minute, forty-seven seconds on the cube. I'm smelling Ivy.

LOVE'S GONE. LOVE NEEDS surgery to repair the damage to his shoulder, then four to six months to recover. Olynyk gets a one-game suspension, which he'll serve next October, for injuring Love and knocking him out of the playoffs The NBA balances this mercy by suspending JR for the Cavs' first two games in the second round.

It doesn't help that the second round is against the Bulls or that the series opens three days before the twenty-sixth anniversary of The Shot, when Michael became Michael and Craig Ehlo, a scrappy, honest journeyman, collapsed into Cleveland sports history.

LeBron himself has ended the Bulls' season all three times they've faced off in the playoffs, but this Chicago team is better, tougher. Joakim Noah talks a lot of shit and backs it up, and Derrick Rose is healthy, and they've got Pau Gasol, and Jimmy Butler, young, hungry, and very good, *wants* to guard LeBron.

And David Blatt is missing 40 percent of his starting lineup. I don't wish to piss on David Blatt, but after eight days of planning—it took the Bulls six games of bear-waltzing with the Bucks to make the second round—Blatt sticks Mike Miller in the starting lineup for Game 1, the team comes out flat, with fifteen first-quarter points, and the crowd, well trained, grows hushed. The Cavs keep it close—they go into the half down by five—but Gasol hits a skein of wide-open looks from the same spot at the top of the key, and Chicago builds a fifteen-point third-quarter lead by the time Blatt figures out how to adjust his defense.

But the loss is on LeBron, who starts rusty and tries to do too much in Love's absence, and never finds his shot. Give Butler credit, too—James turns the ball over six times, twice near the end of the game, when the Cavs still have a chance to pull it out, with Butler on him like a courtroom glove. The Cavs lose, 99-92.

"I have to be better," LeBron says after the game. "I have to be much better."

Yep. He finishes only one assist shy of a triple-double, with fifteen rebounds and nineteen points, but he's LeBron.

I'm driving back to the condo when I hear Blatt's post-game presser.

"We had a shot to win that game," he says, and I turn off the radio right there. I want to drive back to the Q, bribe my way down to the locker room, and snatch him bald. YOU started Miller, jackass, after barely using him all season. YOU stood pat on the sidelines like a deer on I-80 while Gasol hit eight of eight uncontested jumpers on the same goddamned pick-and-pop. Your team just lost home-court advantage for the series in a game it could have won. You sound almost pleased, rookie. Putz.

I'M IN CLEVELAND ALONE because of school, and besides, Judah has a girlfriend now. It starts with a study date on April 12, and it quickly turns into a river of study dates, and the kid is deep in the heart of a land I've only read about and never dared imagine: high school love. I never had a date or studied. I was very fat and angry, and my school was full of greasers, young Italian men, many of them barber-college bound, and young women with dark eye shadow and lacquered hair.

I don't know what I'm supposed to do as a father here. She's a peach, beautiful, smart, and funny. So is he. The town abounds with such shiny goodness—Tom Cruise went to high school here—but I know that it's veneer, artificial turf.

They're sixteen-year-old sweethearts, and biology is biology. I trust the plan—I don't remember the last time he didn't get an A—but I would be derelict in my duty as his father if I didn't discuss his weaponry. I want my son to open his heart wide to love and keep his johnson in his pants. Sanford has four sons, and their sperm runs hot and strong.

They don't drive yet, so one night when I pick him up at her house, I tell him it's time that we talked about the facts of life.

You want face-to-face or e-mail? I'm good either way.

"E-mail," Judah says. "Definitely."

I post it to him the day before I hit the road for the Chicago series. Not my finest work, but it's not a job. Still, I work hard on it. Just one joke, about autoerotic asphyxiation. I stuck to a basic pitch: No Genital Penetration. I'm hoping that I jumped the gun, but I don't want to have to do this in increments. The kid has dealt with a world of sexuality entirely separate from mine—I didn't find out the Hardy Boys were bi until my midthirties—but the biological truth remains: at any age, in any age, foreplay is a one-way street, at least when it comes to those who find themselves cisgender, in so far as I understand that term, which Judah once explained to me.

I text him now to ask if he read my e-mail.

"I did."

And?

"You have nothing to worry about."

Questions?

"I'm good."

I can't believe they lost the opener.

"And what did you expect?"

ON THE OFF-DAY BETWEEN games, I get a little daffy and drive to the far east side of town and purchase three pairs of fine shoes—Allen Edmonds—for more money than I've ever paid for footwear, socks included, in my life. I do this for the same reason Pip licks himself—because I can—and because the kid and I now wear the same size, but there is more to it: LeBron buys shoes here. It sounds creepy, I know, but I don't think of it that way. The shoes are mojo: not mere good luck, but a token of shared power, a symbol—especially the calfskin boots, which I'd never wear, but they'll glow on the kid—of the ultimate unity of the cosmos.

We're in sync, me and LeBron, who comes out blazing for Game 2 and lays waste to Jimmy Butler, slashing and bulling to fourteen first-quarter points on the way to a blowout win. I know even before the game that he's lit: He has his head-band on. He'd ditched it three months ago, for the first time in his career, for reasons unknown and unexplained. Until tonight.

"It was in my locker, and I decided to give it a go," LeBron says. "It was time for it to make a comeback."

Things don't go as well in Chicago. Game 3 is a battle all the way to the final buzzer, when Derrick Rose banks in a twenty-six footer to win the game, 99-96—and just like that the Cavaliers are down two games to one. JR's back, but

Kyrie's limping now, and the headband has a gutty night—twenty-seven points, fourteen assists, eight rebounds—but Rose's shot hits the glass and goes in, and the Chicago crowd goes wild. It's all over but the Blatting.

"Look, we're not talking about it, but Kyrie has been playing hurt," Blatt says after the loss. "He's showing a lot of courage, and he's giving us all he has. He's playing his heart out. He's playing hurt, and I'm proud of him."

That's sweet, but the reason the Cavs aren't talking about it is that it's the playoffs and you're trying to win a championship—and by the way, rookie, this is precisely why smart coaches limit minutes and rest key players *during the regular season*. Kyrie ranks fourth in the league in minutes per game, and he had an awful night—three of thirteen shooting, no assists—but he hasn't said word one about his foot, so shut the fuck up.

"I know Coach was doing that to protect me," Kyrie says. "I don't make any excuses for myself."

Someone asks LeBron if Kyrie gets a pass tonight for zero assists, and pisses him off.

"Don't none of us get a pass," LeBron says. "He gave us forty minutes on one foot. I had seven turnovers tonight. I was eight of twenty-five. Put it on me."

LeBron's also mad at Joakim Noah, for calling him a bitch in a third-quarter tête-à-tête after Noah fouled him hard, off the ball. It is their eighteenth playoff-game meeting, and Noah's sick of losing and having a bad game.

"I'm a father with three kids," LeBron says. "It got very

disrespectful. As a competitor, I love Jo, but the disrespectful words he said to me were uncalled for."

James doesn't repeat Noah's language, but still: Who else in the history of American professional sports talks like this after a killing loss? You leave the moment out there on the floor; you hew to the code. But LeBron's a fucking sage now. He's not just a players' union VP, and a dad, and the greatest basketball player ever. He's fucking Maimonides.

THE CAVS ARE PLAYING for their lives in Game 4. The Bulls have never been up on a LeBron team in the playoffs, their home crowd is thirsting for blood, and if the Cavaliers go down three games to one, with no Love and Kyrie playing on one foot, the season's over.

It's a festival of slop. Kyrie's gimping through another forty minutes, and LeBron rolls an ankle in the third quarter and plays on, badly. But Mozgov, Shumpert, and Tristan are balls-out on D, and JR hits three clutch threes, and the game's tied at eighty-four with nine seconds left, and the Cavs are going to inbound the ball—so they'll get the final shot, and, if it misses, overtime.

Wait! David Blatt wants a time-out, to diagram the game-winning play just like he did in Thessaloniki, and he starts walking onto the court, signaling the TO. What Blatt fails to grasp, beyond the fact that he's a rookie coach choking under playoff pressure, is that the Cavs are out of time-outs, which makes what Blatt's doing a technical foul, which will result in a free throw for the Bulls, followed by possession, likely followed by a loss that'll put the Bulls up 3-1 in the series and all but end Cleveland's season.

It is, no question, the stupidest move I've ever seen a head coach make at any level of play in any sport, and the only reason it doesn't cost the Cavs the game is that none of the three refs, who are fully aware that both teams are out of time-outs, notices Blatt on the court signaling for a time-out before Tyronn Lue, leaping from the Cavs' bench, intercepts the Eurowhiz before any ref spots him.

By Cleveland standards, this is a miracle. Lue, however, neglects to punch Blatt out of his Eurotrance, and so, with one and a half ticks left and the game still tied, the rookie coach finally gets his chance to draw up that game-winning play and offers proof of brain death: Blatt's play is designed for LeBron James to inbound the ball from under the basket.

This is bizarre unto insane. David Blatt has called a play that starts with the greatest player in league history standing out of bounds looking to pass the rock to someone else, with the game tied, one-point-five seconds left, and the Cavs' playoff future at stake. Under NBA playoff pressure, Blatt's pissing down his leg.

King James says no.

"Have somebody else take the ball out and give me the ball and get out of the way."

Blatt switches the play. Matthew Dellavedova, Kyrie's backup, inbounds the ball, hitting LeBron in the corner near the baseline, and James, who has missed twenty shots already in this game, swishes a twenty-footer over Jimmy Butler to win it.

And just for the record, this is LeBron's third career buzzer-beater in the playoffs. In his postseason career, Michael Jordan hit five of eleven go-ahead shots with under five seconds to play; LeBron has now made six of eleven.

If you think Blatt's sheepish after Lue and LeBron rescue his dumb ass, and his job, you're possibly thinking of some other, less haughty, schmuck.

"A near mistake was made," Blatt says after the game, "and I owned up to it, and I own it. A basketball coach makes a 150 to 200 critical decisions during the course of a game, something that I think is paralleled only by a fighter pilot. If you do it for twenty-seven years, you're going to blow one or two, and I blew one. Fortunately, it didn't cost us."

David Blatt, fugue-state fighter pilot, doesn't mention that LeBron vetoed Blatt's moronic last play. LeBron does.

"To be honest, the play that was drawn up—I scratched it. I told Coach just give me the ball and it's either going to overtime or I'm going to win it for us. It was that simple."

No big thing.

"Players make mistakes, coaches make mistakes, and we have to be able to cover for one another."

He isn't Rambam or the Besht. And he isn't Michael Jordan.

He is LeBron James, hoops rebbe.

THE CAVS DON'T LOOK back. Lot's wife is still head coach—I don't know to a certainty that Dan Gilbert would've fired his ass had the Cavs lost the series, though I believe so—but it doesn't matter anymore. I drive to Cleveland overnight for Game 5 and watch LeBron score thirty-eight to lead the Cavs to a win. Kyrie doesn't look like he has a bad left knee and right ankle—he hits for twenty-five—but the high point of the night arrives in the fourth quarter with the Cavs up by ten, when Dellavedova, an undrafted free agent from Australia—one of those scrappy, slow Caucasian fan favorites salting each NBA roster—hits the floor after getting shoved by Chicago's Taj Gibson, clamps his legs around Gibson's ankle and twists it, trying to pull him down. Taj yanks loose his leg, kicks Dellavedova in his ass with it, and gets tossed out of the game.

"I was just trying to get up," Delly says after the win, buck toothed, chipmunk cheeked. "And then a bit of a push and shove."

They're coming together nicely, LeBron's Cavs. And LeBron knows it.

"We just want to play ball," James says postgame. "But we'll protect our brothers."

There is swagger in his voice, and on the court now. JR and Shumpert are bringing it both ways, and on defense and the glass, with Mozgov and Tristan, they're tougher than with Love. They ice the Bulls in Game 6, 94-73—Chicago scores only forty-two total in the last three quarters—and thus far hath LeBron brung us: the Cleveland Cavaliers are in the Eastern Conference Finals.

It is no small thing to see him at the podium flanked by Tristan and Dellavedova. LeBron's in a black leather biker jacket, a wide-brim black fedora low on his head, Thompson's wearing a black topcoat, a dark scarf draped around his neck, Delly's sporting his hooded parka, army green, half-zipped.

LeBron brings whomever he wants with him to these play-off pressers—sitting next to the King up there with all the cameras on you is like getting a game ball or the employee-of-the-month spot in the parking lot. Tristan's up there for his seventeen rebounds and his defense—he has replaced Kevin Love's skills with his own, and his own are perfect for the playoffs. And Delly's there because he's playing for the Cleveland Cavaliers, so naturally Kyrie, who has a bad right foot and left-knee tendinitis, steps backward onto Thompson's foot early in the second quarter, collapses to the floor, and limps off to the locker room, meaning that the kid in the parka, who looks like he runs a Jiffy Lube, is now the Cavs' point guard and plays the best game of his young life, leading the team with nineteen points, one fewer than Derrick Rose, in an elimination game.

Someone asks Delly about halftime, about how it felt knowing he'd have to step up, about what LeBron told him. Delly shrugs.

"Andy grabbed me an extra coffee and said just go out and play. That's about it."

Nobody mentions the fact that LeBron essentially played

the point tonight—he shot like shit, but he posted eleven assists, plus nine rebounds, yet he does these things so routinely, even with the Cavs' subs on the court with him, that his unique genius gets lost in the fog of game-story bullshit.

Tristan Thompson's talking about "being part of the playoffs and having the opportunity to play with this great father over here," looking sideways at LeBron next to him, and LeBron laughs, but not as hard as he laughs a minute later, when some fool asks him if the Cavs might be underdogs facing the Hawks, who won sixty games—including three of four against the Cavs—and will have home-court advantage.

"*Hahhh. Underdog?*" LeBron says. "*ME?*"

Fool says, Well, I don't think so . . .

"*Dahhh*. Me either. I would never be an underdog."

Las Vegas agrees. Strongly.

"GREAT FATHER" IS THE meme du jour. With six whole days until the conference finals start and an infinitude of screens and airtime to fill, paterfamilias becomes a major story line, along with J. R. Smith's struggle toward redemption.

I get it. If there's no game, no news, no controversy, you still have to file something. But these two stories, so positive and warm on their surface, trouble me. Actually, they shame me.

"Kyrie," one questioner begins, "Tristan called LeBron a great father after the Chicago win—"

"He *what*? Oh, a great father. I interpreted that completely wrong. I thought you said he was a great father *to him*."

Kyrie's smiling. It's after practice. He's leaning against a wall, surrounded by the media pack. Both his legs are fucked, and the whispers say that it's a pain-tolerance issue, not an injury, and he can play with it against the Hawks if only he'd man up and grit his teeth—like you-know-who. He isn't expecting this bullshit:

"So what type of parental role has he played for you and your teammates?"

Kyrie lowers his head, touches his hand to his forehead, and hides his eyes for a moment, as if pausing to remind himself that he isn't a little boy, nor fatherless, that no insult was intended, that the question is prompted by needing a quote and phrased as it is out of ignorance. The bond between black athletes and the media is one of mutual contempt and dependency. Irving must answer, not just as a professional basketball player and a young black man and someone's son; he is also Uncle Drew. And he's smart.

"Okay," Kyrie says. "So you—*parental* role?"

He's looking at her now, laughing quietly at her.

"He's been a great leader for us. But I have one father—that's my dad, Drederick Irving."

Kyrie's mother died when he was four years old. His father raised him alone. Kyrie looks down as he names his dad. He sounds solemn as he says the name, in full: Drederick Irving.

A father's name is important to a son.

And when he's asked about JR, what kind of teammate he is, and whether the media cartoon of him is unfair, Irving stays serious.

"Outside looking in, everyone has their own perception. This crazy, outside perception can get ahold of anybody, and then they always have to defend themselves, and then we ask questions like this, that I'm answering. You guys don't go to sleep with me, I don't go to sleep with you guys. You guys don't see me unless I'm on the court. What goes on in our lives is the only thing that matters to me—and it's not defined by you guys. It's defined by me."

These questions and the story lines aren't meant to be demeaning, or racist, but they strike me now as both, and I recoil because of all the years I've spent pretending to own some special insight into famous people's souls, including, in particular, LeBron's. I'm sick of it. I can barely understand myself on a clear day.

Just let the kid get treatment for his legs. If you're desperate for a story line, twelve-year-old Tamir Rice is still dead seven months later, and the city prosecutor is still waiting for the county sheriff to finish investigating a two-second execution by a cop who was let go by a suburban police department because he broke down in tears on the fucking firing range, *BEFORE* he was hired by the CPD.

Hell, I'd do it myself, but what the world *truly* needs now is another white man's sports memoir. Besides, I've got another *Esquire* cover: The Rock. Maybe I'll ask him about his dad.

THE HAWKS ARE ROADKILL. The Cavs smack them twice in Atlanta to open the series. It doesn't even matter that Kyrie's too hurt to play in Game 2; down two of the Big Three, the Cavs still have LeBron. Toughened up by the Celtics and the Bulls, quickened by Shumpert and Thompson jumping out and switching on defense, knowing the mass of Mozgov stands behind them, Cleveland's defense shuts the Hawks down, holding them under ninety points both games.

The kid and I head to the condo for the two games at the Q. It's Memorial Day weekend, the games are Sunday and Tuesday, and if we leave right after Tuesday's game and I can stay awake all night at the wheel, then he'll miss only one day of school.

I might not be able to drive all night after the game, bub.

"I know that."

You might miss two days. Two.

"I know."

You'll still get into a good college. Probably.

"Is that a deer?"

WHAT THE FUCK! God DAMN it, Judah. Don't fuck with me like that.

"What? I thought I saw a deer."

SUNDAY NIGHT'S GAME IS BLISS. All else is window dressing once the ball is tipped; nothing matters, from the game-show bombast of the Q to the noble tribal vision of The Return itself—only the basketball counts. Ball doesn't lie.

Kyrie is on the sidelines in a suit, watching—he tries working out with a new knee brace before the game, but no go—

and LeBron misses his first ten shots, and the Hawks, backed against a wall, play harder than they did at home. The game is ragged nearing halftime, with Atlanta up by one, when Matthew Dellavedova makes mischief once more; battling for a loose ball with Al Horford, the Hawks' six-foot-ten-inch center, Delly falls over another Hawk already on the floor and rolls into Horford's right knee, inspiring Horford, as he tumbles, to drop his arm and elbow onto the back of Delly's neck—hard enough for the refs to review the play once the court is cleared of the fallen.

It is old-school playoff basketball, and our seats are just about perfect—second row of the upper bowl, center court—and the Q's shaking as we stand roaring for the blood of our enemies in the long minutes that pass while the referees study the tape and confer, and the Humongotron endlessly replays the sequence.

The officials do the wise thing: Dellavedova draws a technical foul; they ding Horford with a Flagrant 2 and throw him out of the game. Counting Taj Gibson and the Hawks' sharpshooter Kyle Korver—Delly, diving for a loose ball in Game 2, somehow managed to roll Korver's ankle, spraining it—the Cavs' backup point guard has felled three enemy combatants himself. He's a weapon.

But nothing like LeBron. In the third quarter alone, he scores fifteen points, gathers six rebounds, and adds six assists. And still the Hawks refuse to go down, and LeBron's right leg is cramping as Atlanta claws back from down ten to tie the game, so LeBron bangs home a three with thirty-six seconds left in overtime, then a deuce, and he drops to the court as the clock runs out on a 114-111 Cavs win.

I've never seen anything like the game he had with my own eyes: thirty-eight points, eighteen rebounds, thirteen assists, forty-seven minutes. In fact, no one else has ever put up those numbers in an NBA playoff game; the last time anyone had 35-15-10 was 1993, when Charles Barkley did it in his first Phoenix season.

But that's not news: King James has had better games. The story line is Delly, the Aussie assassin. He's sitting next to LeBron at the podium postgame, wearing the same green winter jacket and what looks like the same black T-shirt underneath it. LeBron's got on a patterned top with half sleeves and white stripes; his hat looks like a Royal Canadian Mountie's, with a band of sparkling gold circling the crown.

The media dutifully frames its questions with quotes from angry Hawks about Delly's "track record," and it's all about boxing out and playing hard until someone asks, "For either of you—when you're out there, what responsibility do you have for the safety of the other nine guys on the floor?"

"What does that mean?" LeBron says.

James knows one thing it means—it means the guy asking has never played a professional sport—and he clearly resents the malice it implies. In fact, the reporter grew up an Atlanta Hawks fan, and he sounds offended by Dellavedova's wanting moral compass. He doesn't come after Delly with a quote from one of his Hawk heroes, fallen or otherwise; he's here to speak on their behalf—and he's swinging the mace of keyboard ethics.

"In terms of style, do you have to be mindful—"

LeBron cuts him off.

"At this point, you do whatever it takes to win. This guy here, people are trying to give him a bad rap—he doesn't deserve it and I don't like it. He comes to play as hard as he can every single night. If they're focused on Delly, they're focused on the wrong thing."

Ball does not lie. The Hawks at full strength are a coach's dream, built on finesse and playbook scheme; they don't rebound, box out, or dive for loose balls like they grew up playing Australian-rules football, and the Cavs are playing without Love and now Kyrie, and LeBron's playing to exhaustion every game, and genteel fanboy morality can go piss up a rope.

IN 116 PREVIOUS PLAYOFF series, no NBA team down three games to none has ever survived to win, and the Hawks had no apparent interest in trying to become the first, so Game 4 is a thirty-point cakewalk.

Kyrie's starting, a surprise and delight to all, including Atlanta, since it means less of the dread Delly, Cleveland's newest folk hero. We're in the same seats tonight, thanks to Dan Gilbert's fantabulous Flash Seats swindle, which allows that asshole to swipe a usurious cut of the inflated resale price of the same playoff tickets the Cavs have already peddled once, and Judah, whose defense on the pitch is not unlike the Aussie axman's, has made a simple sign at a sign-making table in the Q concourse:

OUTBACK JESUS

It's over by halftime, and gee, Kyrie looks swell. Blatt limits him to five-minute stretches, and Kyrie cuts and dekes and feints his way to sixteen points—with five assists and one turnover—in twenty-two tidy minutes. LeBron takes it easy, puts up a near triple-double in twenty-nine minutes—he finishes the sweep three assists shy of *averaging* a triple-double for the series—and the Cleveland Cavaliers are going to make the NBA Finals for the first time since 2007.

My phone starts buzzing with five minutes left in the game—ESPN wants me outside at the corner of Ontario and Huron to do a postgame stand-up with Mark Schwartz. I do not tell them to fuck off, I'm here with my son and we want to see the trophy raised. I'm proud to represent and get paid—and besides, though I'd never say it on-air, *this* trophy means nothing. NOTHING.

The kid brings his sign, and we join Mark Schwartz and a mob of drunken fans, and I shout my hosannas into his microphone—and by the time we get back in the car, it's past midnight.

No way we're making it past Clarion tonight.

"Not a problem," the kid says. World's Greatest Kid—I

got him that trophy, a big one, with wings, for his fourth birthday.

You gonna make it back for the Finals?

"It doesn't look good, bub. I have finals, too."

Game 7, bub. June 19. I already checked—it's a Sunday night.

"We'll see."

13

VIA DOLOROSA

Because I am a two-platform pundit, I must predict a Cavaliers championship for Esquire.com and prepare an ESPN obituary for their defeat. This is a metaphor for nothing. It means next to nothing. It's my job, and I feel strongly both ways. The Cavs are heavy underdogs to the Warriors. Golden State earned the home-court advantage with 67 regular-season wins, more than all but five teams in NBA history, and they are 47-3 at Oracle through the playoffs. They rank first in defense in the league, second in offense, they're healthy, and they have the MVP, of course, plus the heavy-breathing adoration of the metrics geeks.

The Cavaliers have LeBron. Much nattering about his statistical inefficiency: so many missed shots, and the jumper has never looked worse, and the turnovers, and he's aware of it all—talks about it all, in fact. With Kyrie hobbled, missing games, and Love gone, LeBron's options are constrained, and so he's merely averaging twenty-seven, ten, and eight, a playoff stat line last matched by Oscar Robertson in 1963.

Bring them on.

TWO MINUTES LEFT IN overtime, Game 1, Cavs down four, and Kyrie Irving's driving hard across the lane with Klay Thompson riding his left hip. Irving plants his left foot—to stop, to cut, to let Klay fly by—and his left leg buckles. After forty-four minutes of play—twenty-three points, seven rebounds, six assists, four steals, great defense on Curry, even blocking a layup from behind near the end of regulation—Kryie's pain tolerance matters no more: his left kneecap is now fractured.

LeBron's forty-four points aren't enough. Thirty-eight shots, forty-six minutes, another brutal playoff loss: Who knows what awful memories come flooding back to him? So many to choose from. Now this: Kyrie leaving Oracle Arena on crutches.

"It was very tough to see," James says. "That's a tough blow for our team."

Without Kyrie, there is no hope. There is just LeBron.

"We had our chances. We had so many opportunities to win this game and we didn't. It's up to us now to look at the film, watch, and make some adjustments. Be ready for Sunday."

I SHOULD JUST LET him be by now, the dildo David Blatt. He has just coached his first NBA Finals game, and lost in overtime, and lost his point guard and favorite son; his key players are playing nearly every second of the game, and lost and then saw Kyrie needing help to get twelve feet from his locker to the trainer's room after the game, and saw his dad, Drederick Irving, slamming doors, enraged; even with all that, this Eurowizard, this *nar*, finds a way with his mouth to make it worse.

"I thought we came out of regulation flat, without the kind of energy we displayed throughout the game. We sort of dropped off the map a little bit."

Really, motherfucker? I'm so sorry that your players let you down. Maybe you should teach them Eurocourage.

I have never kicked my dog. Never. And now I know I never will.

THE CAVS SLOW THE game—LeBron's walking the ball across court, dribbling in isolation on offense, letting the clock run. They have no other choice to have a chance to win. No Love, no Kyrie: it's simple now. Bron, Mozgov, Thompson, Shump, and Delly, with JR and rusted James Jones off the bench—that's all, folks—against these Nureyevs, who flow ten players deep and cut and slash and run: the Cavs dig in on defense, pound the boards, LeBron's burning time to limit Warriors possessions, and Delly's on Steph and Steph is not used to getting bumped or diving for loose balls. The Cavs are kicking Golden State's ass.

The Warriors rally in the fourth—Kerr goes with a smaller, faster lineup, the better to run the Cavs into the ground—tie it up at 87-87, forcing overtime. With ten seconds left and the Cavaliers down one, Dellavedova rebounds a James Jones airball, gets fouled on the putback, and sinks both free throws to put the Cavs ahead, 94-93. Then Curry misses yet another jumper with Delly in his face, then turns the ball over with two ticks left, and by god the Cleveland Cavaliers have the first Finals win in franchise history.

"It had everything to do with Delly," LeBron says after the game. "He just kept a body on Steph. He made Steph work. He was spectacular, man. We needed everything from him."

The MVP hits five of twenty-three shots—two of fifteen from three and zero, as in zero, of eight with Delly on him—and wonders aloud about his rhythm and mechanics. No one tells Steph that both Derrick Rose and Atlanta's Jeff Teague likewise suffered rhythm and mechanics problems with Outback Jesus guarding them.

LeBron suffers through another inefficient triple-double—thirty-nine points, sixteen rebounds, eleven of the Cavs' fourteen assists. And when the clock runs out, he slams the ball to the court with all his might, pounds his chest, and roars, and I e-mail my guy in Bristol to let him know ESPN won't be needing any fucking obit.

I'VE GOT TICKETS FOR Games 3 and 4 at the Q. Judah stays home to study for finals. Strange, strange kid.

On the road alone again, I'm listening to Zevon, whom I never met but miss very much, and I'm thinking about how this is LeBron's fifth straight Finals appearance, which no other NBA player since Bill Russell's Celtics can say, and with all due respect to Dellavedova and the Cavaliers' defense, James is making myth right now.

After Game 1, after he scores forty-four and loses, LeBron cuts off some media moron who begins his question by saying that the Warriors' defensive strategy was to "let you have forty."

"You don't LET me get forty," LeBron says. "I go GET forty."

And after he go-gets thirty-nine and wins Game 2, LeBron makes sure to bring that bullshit up again.

"Once again, I was knocking on the forty door. So they let me score forty again."

Whatever Golden State's strategy, the Cavaliers are outplaying the Warriors. If LeBron doesn't miss a three at the end of regulation in Game 1, the Cavs are heading home with a 2-0 lead—no Kyrie, no Love, no MVP. Just LeBron.

IN THE MOMENTS BEFORE Game 3 tips off, LeBron turns from the circle to the sideline, stops, points, presses his palms together, and bows low to a big old man dressed in black sitting courtside.

Jim fucking Brown.

Staring at him, barely smiling, the old man brings his own hands up, returning his respect to LeBron James.

I saw this with my own eyes.

LEBRON'S LINE TONIGHT IS forty points, twelve rebounds, eight assists, and four steals in only forty-six minutes—no overtime—and Delly adds twenty, cramping so severely by the end that even an IV isn't enough; he leaves the Q in an ambulance bound for the Cleveland Clinic, where they treat him overnight and disclose, to his dismay, that coffee is a diuretic. Blatt has largely given Tyronn Lue the defensive reins, and the Cavs stifle Golden State to fifty-five through three quarters, weather a late-game Curry eruption, and hang on to win, 96-91.

Through three Finals games, with Dellavedova as the Cavs' second scoring option—JR is not open often, and not hot when he is—LeBron's averaging forty-one points and eight assists versus an elite defense, and controlling the pace and flow almost every minute of every game. I don't know how much longer he can keep this up. I don't know how the Cavs can keep grinding playing seven guys while the Warriors are rotating ten, and I don't know if I should buy myself a ducat for Game 5 in Oakland—in case LeBron James should just happen to raise a trophy that night.

What I do know:

- LeBron James got 5 of 130 first-place votes for league MVP, finishing third.
- The Cavaliers are two wins away.
- LeBron bowing to Jim Brown was some Homeric shit.

Its import wasn't lost on Jim Brown, who walks with a cane and still looks like he could hurt you with a glare.

"It was an honor for this young man to pay tribute to an old soldier," Brown says. "It was one of my favorite sports moments of all time. I'll be eighty in February, and that's a lot of years. To have a young man think of me during the pressure he was going through—the pressure of that type of game—it's a wonderful honor."

STEVE KERR DESERVES A book of his own—suffice it to say that when he played, he played at the Hall of Fame end of the scrappy-white-guy continuum, with a sweet three-point stroke that proved impervious to playoff pressure when he joined Michael Jordan's Bulls; in his fifteen-year career—including an early stint in Cleveland, before the Cavs traded him for a second-round pick—Kerr won three rings as a Bull and two more as a Spur, and retired at the age of thirty-seven as the most accurate long-distance shooter in NBA history.

Steve Kerr has had a day to think it over. He pulls Andrew Bogut, a seven-foot Australian who's being outplayed down low by Blatt's seven-foot Russian, and starts Andre Iguodala, a six-foot six-inch swingman, quick and strong, instead. Mozgov has to come out to guard him—Iguodala hits four open threes—and that opens the lane for the Warriors to cut and drive.

It's Andre Iguodala's first start of the entire season, and it's a brilliant move. He's guarding LeBron close, making him work, and the Warriors are doubling more, bringing help, so

LeBron's passing off—to Mozgov, freed of Bogut underneath, and to Delly, JR, and Shump, out at the three-point arc.

All that's working is Mozgov. Shumpert hurt his shoulder in Game 3; he's shooting with one arm. Delly can't hit. JR's shot is a catastrophe. Golden State's racing into transition on long rebounds off the misses, running the Cavs ragged.

With five minutes left in the first half and the Cavs down eleven, LeBron's fouled going to the hoop, stumbles, and dives into a still-photographer's camera, gashing his head. It is no metaphor—it's real blood.

He brings the Cavs back in the third, almost, plays every minute of the quarter, scores ten points, cuts the lead to six when Kerr calls a time-out to yell at his team.

"THEY'RE PLAYING SEVEN GUYS. THEY'RE GONNA WEAR DOWN."

You know what David Blatt yells at his guys?

"SPRINT BACK!"

I guess he feels that Cavs aren't running fast enough. Or is it that these NBA poseurs lack the stamina of EuroLeaguers? LeBron's gassed, but when he comes out, the Cavs collapse; he comes back, under two minutes later, and goes scoreless the rest of the way. The Cavs miss sixteen of their eighteen fourth-quarter shots. JR hits zero of eight three-pointers, Dellavedova two of nine, and the Warriors win it going away, 103-82.

LeBron's on the bench to finish the game, with 20-12-8 and stitches in his head. It's their third game in five nights, and they're cooked. Blatt has no answers for Kerr's depth—he had no use for the old heads most of the season; though, to be fair, Jones, Miller, and Marion had no use for Blatt, either, and they'd be of little use against the Warriors without the help of time travel.

It's a best-of-three series now, Golden State hosts two of them, and the Cavs are down to one player, and while I feel certain that he is the best basketball player I've ever seen, I need to take a second run at that obit.

It's only sports. Only sports. Only sports.

STEPH CURRY, ANGEL INCARNATE, puts on an MVP show in Game 5, with thirty-seven points and seven threes. LeBron goes triple-double again, with 40-14-11 in forty-five minutes, and it's not enough. Not even close. The Cavaliers hang close for a half—Blatt pulls Mozgov, trying to go small to match Steve Kerr's Bogutless Lineup of Death, but JR goes colder than Ted Williams's head, Delly's a pumpkin again, Curry gets seventeen in the fourth, and the Warriors win, 104-91.

Sunday night—tomorrow's the kid's sixteenth birthday. It's only sports. No man is *mastur* of his bate. Just one other player in NBA history ever owned a forty-point triple-double in the Finals—not Michael, but Jerry West, forty-six years ago. Not that that matters now. Fuck it and fuck me—it's all over but the ESPN obit, and I'll head upstairs later and finish that piece of shit.

"We're going home with a Game 6 and we've got enough

to win it," LeBron says at the postgame presser. "We protect home—we come back here."

A deep thinker asks him if he's feeling less pressure "as opposed to previous years" because the Cavs are undermanned, and whatever the hell he means, LeBron doesn't like the question.

"No. I feel confident because I'm the best player in the world. It's that simple."

Game 6 is Tuesday night. I'll take the six a.m. United flight to Cleveland, fly back early Wednesday.

You wanna come?

"I have to study."

Tomorrow's your birthday, man.

"I still have to study."

Game 7?

"We'll see."

He's just humoring me at this point, and we both know it. I go up to the office, finish the obit, and buy myself a ticket for 6 and another one for 7. Not because I think they're going to win 6, but because I just want to see LeBron keep playing basketball—and because I know, like every Cleveland fan my age, that the Cavs may never come so close again, with or without Bron.

IT WAS A MISTAKE to wear the new wingtips, but I have to wear an Izzy suit on the plane because I'm scheduled to do a SportsCenter hit at the ESPN stage on East Fourth Street—

the Cavs still won't give me a credential—and I have to look good or at least my best, and because it is TV, I must flash energy and cheer. I'm going to eat a fancy lunch with my broadcast agent, and I'm going to make back all my game-ticket expense and more on a Wheel of Fortune slot at Dan Gilbert's casino, and the best player in the world is going to tripdub again, and California, here I fucking come.

SportsCenter's fun. I'm sitting with the anchors at a desk up on a stage in the middle of the block, surrounded by the day-drunk mob of Cleveland fans—my people. I assure them that LeBron's got this.

Lunch is long and good. I drop a couple of bills at the casino—the game doesn't start until nine—and get panhandled by a woman needing bus fare. I've been inside seedy casinos—I spent a week in Laughlin, Nevada, twice—but she's my first beggar.

She seems unimpressed, even scornful, when I cite the cost of tuition at Princeton.

That thing I was feeling—survivor's remorse? Fuck that, too. It's guilt. I should just give her the shoes, because by the time I wind up at the casino, I've walked downtown all day with the stiffened counter of my right shoe gouging my heel until it finally slices through the sock and into my flesh. Each step burns, there's still an hour before tip, and my pant leg is now stuck to my bloody Achilles, which turns out to be a handy metaphor for the Cavaliers.

The game is more of the same. The Cavs keep it close for a

half, but the Warriors are running, hitting threes, and pick-and-rolling poor Mozgov to exhaustion in their half-court offense. The Warriors pull away in the third—their depth and balance is amazing, their defense quick and rugged, their hair perfect.

Cleveland has no answer but LeBron, who plays an ungodly forty-seven minutes and sits for an hour at his locker with a towel over his head before he goes to meet the press.

Thirty-two points. Eighteen rebounds. Nine assists. And another Finals loss—his fourth, as many Finals series losses as Michael Jordan, Kobe Bryant, and Larry Bird combined, in twelve fewer Finals appearances. LeBron led both teams in points, rebounds, and assists—he averaged 36-13-9—the first player ever to do so in the NBA Finals. Without him on the floor, JR, Dellavedova, Shumpert, and James Jones take twenty-one shots over six games and make not a single one, and Golden State wins the last three games of the series by an average of fourteen points.

For all his forty-five minutes per game of herculean heroics, LeBron earns four votes for Finals MVP. Iguodala, averaging 15-5-4 in thirty-seven minutes per game, garners seven votes, including those of the *Akron Beacon Journal*'s Cavs beat writer and an ESPN reporter working on a column excoriating James for "emasculating" David Blatt.

When he finally makes his way to the media room, LeBron barely looks up. Tonight's hat, a scoutmaster number in a cocoa suede, hides his eyes.

"It's never a success when you go out losing," he says. "Would I rather not make the playoffs or lose in the Finals—I don't know."

He looks up, face slack and sad, voice full of pain.

"I'm almost starting to be—I'd rather not even make the playoffs than lose in the Finals. It would hurt a lot easier."

King James never was a good loser; I always loved him for that. After Orlando beat the Cavs in the 2009 Eastern Conference Finals, he left the court without shaking hands. The media trashed him for that; he had a five-word explanation:

"You don't accept losing, ever."

Tonight he came out of the game with ten seconds left, and made sure, on his way to the bench, to hug Steph Curry and shake Steve Kerr's hand. But he's defiant in his postgame praise.

"I cannot remember a team like them—being healthy all year. We had a lot of talent sitting in suits—I've had a lot of playoff runs and I've been on both sides, and I know one thing: you've got to be healthy, you've got to be playing great at the right time, and you've got to have a little luck. We were playing great, but we had no luck, and we weren't healthy."

Then someone asks if returning to Cleveland was all he thought it would be.

"My family's happy—it makes my job a lot easier. For the fans, I go out there and just try to leave it out on the floor and I hope it's enough."

Let's see: three forty-point games, two triple-doubles—

three but for a lone assist—and that moment on Olympus with Jim Brown. Not to mention the return of hope.

Yessir. I'd call that enough.

DAVID BLATT. David BLATT. DAVID BLATT. He starts with a half-minute encomium to Golden State, which is fine, then come the Blattitudes.

"Not every story has a happy ending—it doesn't mean it's a bad story. This was not. It was a good story. We were in the NBA Finals, two games away from winning it. I think we did pretty well."

Ugh.

When he's asked about coaching LeBron, Blatt chooses his words slowly, hesitating between phrases as if crossing a minefield in Bosnia-Herzegovina.

"He has become a great leader of his team. He was of great assistance to me in many, many ways. And it's an honor to coach him."

His team. Not *this* team. Not *our* team. His team. Sounds right. I don't know. It's over. It doesn't matter. No championship. No book. I should just hit the road, but it's late and I'm tired and hungry, so I head back to the Liberty Bell to clean the seeping gash in my foot. On the way, I grab two Circle K chicken wraps—lunch was beef-cheek pierogi, followed by scallops—and two seltzers, one to wash them down, one to clean my leaking, throbbing gash.

WORK

That's all a man can do: work. Seven out of ten thousand varsity high school basketball players reach the NBA, and behind them come ten thousand more, younger, playing AAU ball, hungry, dreaming, all working their butts off to land one of those seven jobs.

My job, too. Young writers reach out for guidance and inspiration, and I do my level best to discourage them. Most of them are graduates of journalism school and, coddled there by ninnies, they're feeling special, even after five or six internships, still in a rush to reach their goal, which is my job.

It's a job. It's a *job*. Write and read—books, motherfucker, books—and hope your day, or prince, will come. Work at your craft. Be true to your game. Find your voice. It takes forever.

I don't know what else to say. I've had the same job with the same prince since 1992. I don't go to an office. I don't go to parties in New York City. I don't teach. I'm an old guy with a young son in a leafy North Jersey suburb. I know how I got here—and I know it's almost time for me to go.

I'm a relic. There are no more jobs like mine, not for anyone, and I'm a salaryman myself, a celebrity hack running out the clock. I live through younger, abler men. LeBron. My son.

I don't wish to whine, because the thrill is not entirely gone—the week after the Finals, I drive down to Raleigh to visit with Keith Richards—but I can't believe I was born to interview celebrities to fill the pages between cologne ads. I can't believe I have any future at ESPN, and they confirm that by not picking up my option. I can't believe I'm going to live forever, and I can't believe I'll ever die.

I trust the evidence of things seen: LeBron comes home and—Nike ads, essays, Blatt, and all—walks his righteous path, and it is not enough. He could not foresee the Warriors—no one did: They were a fifty-one-win team last season, losing to the Clippers in the first round of the playoffs, with the same roster and Mark Jackson coaching. They hire Kerr—and Curry, Klay, and Draymond Green, five years younger than LeBron, mature—and now folks are talking dynasty.

They're right. LeBron is one year older, and the whispers and rumors speak of his displeasure with Irving and Love: They're selfish. They don't work hard enough, they don't know what it takes to win it all. I don't know what to believe beyond the fact of his return, and the joy I took in it, and, as ever, the sorrow of a season-ending loss.

For all I know, Blatt's right: It's a good story. Maybe now that he's not a rookie, David Blatt will be a better NBA coach, and LeBron trustful, and Kyrie and Kevin will rehab their injuries and work harder at their craft, and the Cavs will scratch and claw and fight their way back to the Finals, and lose to Golden State again.

I CAN STAND THE LOSING, obviously. I've embraced it for so many years that it has defined me—a large part of me, too large—and I feel guilt for inflicting it on my son, and I have pondered all of this ad nauseam, year after year, and here I am, still mired in the same old Cleveland slough of sports despond.

That's all fine. It connects me to my roots. It connects me to my son. Played well, sports as performance art are dazzling; throw in all the feeling, frame it in a familiar narrative, and you have catharsis, Art with a capital *A*. I fucking love it. I always will. I make no apology for any of that.

But I'm having a hard time with Chief Wahoo, the ignoble logo inked into my arm—I got tattooed with Dennis Rodman in 1994, and we were plastered—and the Browns' owner is a carpetbagger whose truck-stop empire practiced fraud for years, and now Dan Gilbert's canoodling with Chris Christie, New Jersey's elephantine shitbag of a governor. Christie was at the Q for Game 3 of the Finals, and, six weeks later, Gilbert donated 750 grand to the venal bastard's PAC.

Dan's hosting the Republicans next summer at the Q, because $4 billion, an NBA team, and casinos aren't enough juice, not for Dan, to whom I have forked over nearly $15,000 this season, not counting the slots.

How many of my own soft-wrung dollars went to that thug Christie?

God DAMN it.

There are times when it's sufficient to invoke Art to reconcile the irreconcilable—why else bother majoring in English if you can't bullshit through this brazen world?—but there are other times, like now, when the map of right and wrong can't be fogged by pretty poetry, when naked truth can claim no beauty prize:

Dan Gilbert will do whatever it takes to win.

That's all I know, and all I need to know.

LEBRON'S NOT GOING ANYWHERE. He signs another two-year deal, retaining the option to leave after one. Kevin Love gets a max deal, five years, $110 million. Shumpert gets four years and $40 million. Tristan Thompson, whose agent is LeBron's agent, holds out all summer, misses training camp, and inks a new contract—five years, $82 million—five days before the season opener. Dellavedova, a restricted free agent, gets one more year and a bump to sixty bucks a game plus a case of Foster's.

Whatever it takes. On top of his cap-busting payroll, Dan Gilbert's forking over an extra $54 million under the NBA's luxury-tax penalty, designed to brake overspending owners, lest the other billionaires go ape. Dan doesn't give a shit. LeBron's salary will be a shade under $23 million, and the estimated value of Gilbert's franchise doubled—from half a billion dollars to a billion—with The Return.

So tell me again: Who's running the Cavs?

LeBron?

I think not. Blatt's making $3 million, and he's still the head coach.

Tell me all about LeBron's selfishness, his failure to buy in, to pay respect to the authority and acumen of David Blatt, to sacrifice the last years of his career to an owner with a meth-head's attention span and a classic Napoleon complex.

Tell me. I'm all ears. I wrote *The Whore of Akron*.

THE CAVS OPEN IN Chicago, and President Obama's coming, and LeBron's excited.

"He loves the game of basketball. We all know that. It's an honor for me to be part of a venue and a spectacle the president would like to come and watch."

Last week, LeBron and Michelle Obama met in Akron to talk about his scholarship program, and an adult GED program he's sponsoring, and a new, federally funded mentorship program, My Brother's Keeper. King James is a *macher* now, a *groiseh k'nocker*, and a movie star—his *Trainwreck* turn shows far more range than Michael's stiffitude in *Space Jam*—and still he's the earnest kid from West Akron who made good, busting with pride.

"Our league is the greatest league in the world. We have the greatest athletes and the greatest fans. So for the president of the United States to grace us on opening night—I'm just honored. It's something I can tell my kids a long, long

time from now. I'll actually be able to show them the film—
the president was at a ball game I played in. That's pretty
cool."

The kid from Princeton, David Blatt, is less impressed. He's
tight with Netanyahu, after all, won that bronze in 2012 for
Putin—Obama's no big whoop for über-Euromensch, and,
when asked if he's coaching in front of the president for the
first time, Blatt takes the question as an opportunity to remind everyone that David Blatt's no rookie when it comes to
heads of state.

"I've been in front of some presidents in other parts of
the world, actually, so—of the United States? Yes. Unless the
president was at the Olympic Games and I didn't know it."

The Cavs lose, 97-95. Kevin Love's healthy, with a cute
new perm, to boot, but Kyrie's knee won't be good to go until December, and Shumpert's mending after wrist surgery.
LeBron looks great, and Blatt appears to have learned how
not to play him forty minutes. But I'm amazed at what Blatt
obviously hasn't even begun to learn.

The NBA is a players' league, unlike the NFL, where brain-
battered chattel sign nonguaranteed contracts, belong to a
players' union unworthy of the name, and are ruled by a lying
dunce of a commissioner, and Major League Baseball, where
no single star can dominate game after game. The NBA is a
superstars' league, and it is indisputably a black league, with
a full range of male, African American experience.

An NBA locker room after a win is a panoply of soul,
from the music and laughter to the language and the accents

and the lotions. The game itself has an inherent tension between the creativity and improvisational skills of the athletes and the system imposed by the coaches. The paradigm so beloved by media and fans—embodied by Pop and Phil and Riles and Red—is still a wise white man, a figure of unquestioned authority, gentle or fierce, schooling his boys, shaping them into the mold of his design.

It can work. It does work. But working it requires an NBA head coach, whatever his style or system, to earn his players' respect and trust. Especially his best player's—the guy he's honored to coach.

It's not necessary, nor is it fair, to ascribe disrespect or racism to Blatt's dismissal of Obama's presence; his profound ignorance and arrogance may well explain it all. But David Blatt showed no respect, or any understanding of what Barack Obama means to anyone but David fucking Blatt. That's a bigger problem than playing time, and I don't know if anyone in the Cavaliers' front office understands that, but I'm fairly certain LeBron James does.

BY MID-NOVEMBER—THE ELEVENTH GAME of the season, a loss to the Pistons—the Cavs sit at 8-3, Golden State 12-0, and LeBron is angry at his team, which gave away a thirteen-point second half lead tonight, and lost in double overtime against the Bucks last time out.

"We haven't done anything," James says. "We didn't win anything. We lost. We lost in the Finals. We didn't win.

And the team that beat us looks more hungry than we are. It shouldn't be that way."

They're soft on D—again. Mozgov had microscopic knee surgery in the off-season and looks slow and lost. JR's awful on both ends of the court. To bridge the Kyrie gap, the Cavs have signed old friend Mo Williams, the choke artist whose dismal three-point shooting sank the Cavs against the Magic in the 2009 ECF, and Mo has never had much interest in playing defense.

"We have the ability to be a great team," LeBron says. "Right now, we're not a very good team."

Different season, same crap. When Kyrie comes back on December 20, with twelve points in seventeen minutes in a romp over the Sixers, the Cavs are 18-7, and on a six-game roll. Five days later, on Christmas, they start a four-game road trip against the Warriors, and with their Big Three together for the first time facing Golden State, they lose, 89-83. Kyrie, Love, and LeBron take fifty-seven shots combined and make nineteen.

Most of the chatter afterward is positive—good defensive effort, just a cold-shooting Christmas Day on the road, plus Blatt's still juggling the rotations with Shumpert and Kyrie back but playing limited minutes. No big deal.

"We play like that defensively," LeBron says, "we're going to be a very tough team to beat."

Even better: Young Uncle Drew's feeling fire in his belly.

"We want what they have," says Kyrie. "We're not stopping until we go get it."

This I like to hear. It helps block out the fact that Golden State's now 28-1. I've seen most of their games on the League Pass, to my horror. Motherfuckers got the chip, then got even *BETTER.*

SOMETHING HAPPENED IN OAKLAND, something mysterious and bad, because the next day, against Portland, the Cavaliers go Lordstown 1972 on Blatt's ass, barely going through the motions, losing to a 12-19 Blazers team missing Dame Lillard by twenty-nine points, 105-76.

Kyrie's sitting, because his kneecap isn't ready for back-to-backs—but there's nothing nuanced about the collective lack of effort: nobody's defending, no one's passing, nobody's running or cutting hard, and nobody's hitting shots. It's 34-12—TWELVE—after the first quarter, and it goes downhill from there. At the half, it's 63-34, against a weak-ass team on a five-game skid.

LeBron himself finishes with twelve points—for the entire game. After he misses his first four shots of the game, he peels off his elbow sleeve while he's in the game and flips it into the Portland crowd, as eloquent a "fuck this" as I've ever seen.

"Offensively, we are in a funk right now," James says afterward. "Our energy was lacking at the beginning. It picked up, but at some point it got so out of hand that it didn't matter. There was nothing good we did tonight. Throw it in the trash."

Then, quietly, he calls out David Blatt.

"We have no rhythm. We have some guys who don't know if they're going to play, and it's hurting our rhythm. For the first eight weeks, we had built chemistry, we knew who was playing, Coach had rotations down—we got to get back to that. We have no rhythm."

It was a wildcat strike. Against Golden State, Blatt shrank his rotation down playoff style and benched Richard Jefferson, one of LeBron's new old heads—a thirty-six-year-old swingman with more left in his tank than the departed Marion and Miller, who signed with the Cavs over the summer for the veteran minimum, hoping for the first ring of his fifteen-year career.

Blatt has played him every game so far this season, until Golden State on Christmas Day, when Jefferson sits out the entire game. Without a word of warning or explanation from David Blatt. That's the proximate cause. The underlying issue is that Blatt faces tough decisions on his rotations with the Cavs back to full strength. LeBron knows that. Jefferson does, too—he played two and a half seasons for Popovich, and he's a respected NBA veteran. Dallas, his last team, wanted him back, but he chose to come play with LeBron, and now he's benched on Christmas Day, when his own family and friends have gathered to watch—and the boss can't even pay him the respect of a heads-up?

I know: They're players—spoiled, whiny children. Millionaires, for heaven's sake. And Blatt's the head coach, the daddy under whose roof they're living, the man in charge. Screw your feelings, sonny—you're getting paid either way.

I've heard this nonsense all my life, and it's reflected in the attitude Blatt brought with him to the NBA. It ain't working. To the minimal extent that he ever truly had them on his side, David Blatt has lost the Cavaliers.

THE YEAR ENDS UGLY all around. The Cavs are 21-9, but Golden State's an absurd 30-2, and in the real world, the Cuyahoga County prosecutor, Timothy McGinty, having gone to great lengths to load the dice, announces that the grand jury he empaneled won't press charges against the cops who murdered Tamir Rice thirteen months ago.

The Cavs are still on the road, in Denver, when LeBron's asked about Tamir, and already #NoJusticeNoLeBron has been endorsed by Black Lives Matter, and activists are publicly calling for him to sit out games in protest.

"To be honest," LeBron says, "I haven't really been on top of this issue, so it's hard for me to comment."

And then LeBron proceeds to comment, in locutions so tortured I want to weep.

"I think the most important thing that we all need to understand, this issue is bigger than LeBron. This issue is bigger than me—it's about everyone. Gun violence and tragedies and kids losing lives, we need to understand that that matters more than just an individual."

Ouch. Listen, I'm no believer in the Great Man theory of human history, and I never mistook LeBron for Malcolm or Martin. But the guy has stood up and spoken out, put money where his mouth is—and if he has no quick take ready after the last game of a weeklong holiday road trip, that doesn't bother me nearly as much as what that clown of a prosecutor did, or as much as a columnist in the New York *Daily News*, who throws this down:

"It's no wonder that police and prosecutors of Cleveland think they can do whatever they want to black folk in the city and get away with it. The most powerful man in town doesn't even care enough to put even a smidgeon of fear in them."

Far be it from the white asshole who wrote *The Whore of Akron* to judge the columnist, Shaun King, for his contempt. King's an activist, not just a writer, and an African American man who has raised money for Tamir Rice's family. I just think his assertion that LeBron James bears any responsibility—past, present, or future—for the way injustice is administered in Cleveland is wishful unto silly.

Of course, that could just be me, getting old. Never mind any cynicism or existential dread; it's fear and despair I'm feeling now. I have stared deep into America's squinting eyes, last month, across the desk from Donald Trump, who declared his candidacy on the day the Warriors won the championship at the Q.

It's clear by now that Trump is a far greater threat to the republic than ISIS, a fucking hood ornament on a bus carrying millions of stupid, angry, racist, misogynistic barnyard animals, many of them heavily armed, each of whom has a vote that counts the same as mine. They don't want a head coach; they want a Führer, and marching orders, and they're wallowing in his innate cruelty as Trump bullies and crushes the cowards, including the gutless Chris Christie, standing in his way.

LeBron can't save the next Tamir Rice, and I can't spare my nation from its fate.

LISA AND I SPEND New Year's Eve alone for the first time since 1999. Judah's with his girlfriend at a party. He's on a nice roll. The soccer team knocks off the one-seed at sectionals, one-nil, and the kid meets an attacking forward at the sideline with a Dellavedovian bump, dislocating his opponent's shoulder and warming the cockles of what's left of my heart. His honey puts the shot, so he goes out for winter track, and the first time I see him sprint, a fifty-five-meter heat at a huge meet on Staten Island, I'm stunned by his speed. He finishes fourth in a field of nine, not that it matters after he wins a 300-meter heat. His time isn't fast enough to qualify for the finals, but that doesn't matter, either—he just found his sport.

I'm in awe, bub. I knew you were fast—not *that* fast.

"My time should've been better. I forgot to lunge at the finish."

Your speed comes from my side, you know. Many of my people ran from Cossacks.

"No doubt."

Seriously, I've never seen a Jew go that fast. Can I call you Kike Lightning?

"Yeah, no."

Judah is my hero, if I have one. I admire him. I envy him a little. I'm going to miss him a lot when, *kinehora*, he goes to college. This is, I know, the natural order of things, and I love my wife very much, and I'm looking forward to the rest of our lives—but the rest of our lives is coming right up, and the shot clock's dwindling on fatherhood and everything else.

THE WARRIORS STRUT INTO town on January 18, with Steph wondering out loud whether the visitor's locker room will still smell of the Champagne the Warriors popped last June.

"Walking in that locker room, it'll be good memories," says Wardell Stephen Curry, bronze cherub.

The Cavs find this disrespectful, but the ball, always, is incapable of mendacity. Golden State trashes the Cavs, 132-98. At one point, the Cavs are down by forty-three, the largest deficit any team of LeBron's has ever faced. Curry goes for thirty-five points in twenty-eight minutes; LeBron, with Iguodala on him, scores sixteen. Love takes five shots, hits one, and the Warriors clown him over and over with pick-and-rolls, until Blatt's forced to pull him. Irving can't—or won't—stay with Curry on his cuts; neither can Delly. JR gets to the Q late, plays angry, and rams Harrison Barnes so hard on a pick that he draws a suicide-by-cop Flagrant 2, and gets thrown out of the game. All in all, it's uglier than the Great Portland Laydown.

"Tonight was an example of how far we've got to go to get to a championship level," LeBron says postdisgrace. "We've got a long way to go."

Forget about it. In the Finals, without Love and Irving, the Cavaliers fought on with unity, focus, and effort. They are a team with none of that spirit now. I can tell because Kevin Love is more sulky than usual.

"We have a lot of things to get better at," Love says after the game. "That's going to take a lot of guys looking at themselves in the mirror, and it all starts with our leader over there."

He's nodding, nodding over toward King James.

FOUR DAYS LATER, AFTER back-to-back wins and an explanation from Love that he wasn't blaming LeBron, just affirming his leadership, David Griffin finally fires David Blatt and replaces him with Tyronn Lue. Not as an interim replacement— as the Man.

"I am more than confident," Griffin says, "that [Lue] has the pulse of our team and that he can generate the buy-in required to start to refine the habits and culture that we've yet to build."

Aha! Yes, David Griffin. Yes. Chopin to my ears.

"I'm in our locker room a lot, and there's just a lack of spirit and connectedness right now that I couldn't accept. We've been a group of tremendous individual talent—with individual hopes and dreams. That's not a winning formula. I'm judging a lot more than wins and losses."

Yes, you are, David Griffin. The Cavs are 30-11, the best team in the East, and half the season's already gone.

"Are our hearts, minds, and souls in what we're doing? Are we all in on this? Are we OF this?"

Whoa. I want to join a men's group with you, David Griffin—twice a week. I want to show you my ticket stub, read you my book, hug you, and smell your ginger head.

Griffin tells the media that he didn't consult any of the Cavs before making the decision, knowing full well that nobody will believe him. The first question he takes starts by citing LeBron's reputation as a coach killer.

"I've had problems with this narrative," Griffin says. "LeBron plays for this team, and he's the leader of this team. LeBron does not run this organization. LeBron is *ABOUT* this organization, he is *OF* this organization, and he is *OF* this community, but the narrative that we're taking direction from him—it's just not fair. It's not fair to him, in particular."

All right, then. Good job, Griff. Good effort.

The next day after practice, LeBron meets the press.

"LeBron, you are the face of this team," one reporter says. "You know that people believe that this would not have happened without your say-so."

King James looks somber. You could grow soybeans in the furrows of his brow.

"That's not my concern," LeBron says. "I found out just

like every other player on this team, at three thirty yesterday. I can't get caught up in what other people think—I stopped that a long time ago."

You did, Bron. And you're welcome.

SIX DAYS LATER, I learn that the Hearst Corporation is firing David Granger, my head coach since 1992, and my friend—a man of integrity, vision, and grit, who also kept my family fed. I'm not sure I can be *OF Esquire* without Granger running it, and there's fresher, younger talent out there, some of it not white or male, praying for one shot. Nineteen years at *Esquire*: I'm good. No man is master of his fate—you've got to be healthy, LeBron sayeth, and you need some good luck—but above all, you have to know when to say good-bye. Push comes to shove, I go back to selling shoes.

IN DAVID BLATT'S DEFENSE, he didn't hire himself. Dan Gilbert and David Griffin had no inkling in June 2014 that LeBron would come home; although the Heat had already lost the Finals to the Spurs—and LeBron would become a free agent on July 1—no one with the Cavs seemed to even consider the possibility.

Lue interviewed twice for the Cavs job, and Gilbert and Griffin loved him, but Blatt had head coach experience, albeit minor league, and Lue didn't. They hired Lue as associate head coach with Blatt's consent, and Blatt was glad to put Lue in charge of the defense.

In LeBron's defense, he didn't bond with Lue due to anti-Semitism or disrespect for David Blatt; James has known Lue since high school, played against him as a pro, considers him a friend. He calls Lue "T-Lue" and Blatt "Blatt," though to be fair, everyone calls Blatt that, including T-Lue and, I'm willing to bet, Blatt's wife.

Griffin's not lying when he denies that LeBron runs the franchise, or Blatt would've been dragged out behind the barn long ago, and rightly so. Lue has two rings from his early days with Kobe and Shaq and Phil Jackson with the Lakers; he played with Jordan in DC; he's a hard-nosed kid—turns out everyone's a hard-nosed kid from somewhere—born and raised in Mexico, Missouri, a six-foot-tall point guard who carved out an eleven-year career, mostly coming off the bench, for seven NBA teams. Phil Jackson matched him up with Iverson in the 2001 Finals, and it's worth watching—not least to see Iverson, regal in his swagger, draining a J and then high-stepping over a fallen Lue.

Iverson won the film clip; Lue got a ring.

Unlike Blatt, Tyronn Lue doesn't parry with reporters over word choice when a question doesn't tickle him. Lue answers.

"Me and Bron were friends before, when I played. I talked to Bron, and I told him, 'I've got to hold you accountable. It starts with you—if I can hold you accountable, in front of the team, everybody else got to fall in line.'"

After retiring, Lue was Doc Rivers's enforcer as an assistant with the Celtics and the Clippers—"I was the bad guy when guys would do things wrong. Me and Blake would get into it, me and CP, me and KG"—and sure enough, when LeBron starts chirping at Love during a time-out, Lue barks.

"Shut the *FUCK* up," he says to King James. "I've got this."

And lo and behold, LeBron shuts up.

LUE WANTS THEM TO speed up the offensive tempo, push the ball upcourt, and it's plain right away, when Irving, Love, and LeBron all need a blow early in Lue's first quarter as head coach, that he also wants to shake them awake.

"I think we got tired," Lue says after the Cavs lose. "I just don't think we're in good enough shape right now to play in the style that we want to play."

LeBron concurs, paying respect.

"Yep. We got to get in better shape. If he wants us to play faster, and you want to be out on the floor, you can't get tired, and if you do, you got to come out. Something that Coach Lue wants us to do, and we all got to accept it."

They win ten of their next twelve, scoring a ton, burying the Spurs and Thunder, but there's still only one ball, and LeBron and Kyrie both want it in their hands, and Love—whose "faster" is especially unfast in Lue's up-tempo offense—droops behind the three-point line, waiting, like Dion in the bad old days, for the pass that never comes.

"Kevin has to understand, it's gonna be a sacrifice," Lue

says. "Guys got to play harder, got to get back on defense, got to move the ball. Those three guys got to learn to play together. They got to learn to sacrifice."

It's the same tune LeBron has sung since he came back, and no different in essence from Blatt's. They're soft, Irving and Love—and Shumpert, flush with his fresh deal, has to be told by David Griffin to focus less time on new side projects in music and fashion, and more on the game he gets paid to play. Lue has Thompson at center now—Mozgov's struggling with his knee and his confidence—LeBron at power forward, small forward, center, and point guard, with Kyrie off the ball and hating it.

When they're good, the Cavs look great, tearing up the Spurs and Clippers, but on too many nights Love and Irving get lit up on defense—word is, Kyrie's fretful about his healed knee—and King James looks uninterested, and they're losing to teams they'd crush like grapes, if only they could muster the energy and effort. It's not quite Blatt redux—the offense is better, the defense worse—but this is stuff no coach or GM's pretty words can force on a willful, selfish player.

In late February, the Cavs pick up Channing Frye—a solid playoff move, another, taller Richard Jefferson, a savvy, well-respected vet with a reliable three-point shot—but Gilbert finagles it into a three-way deal so he can dump Varejão and his salary on Portland, saving himself $10 million in luxury taxes.

Waived immediately by the Blazers, Varejão—"One of the heartbeats of our team," says LeBron—signs on with the

Warriors, followed by a series of cryptic LeBron tweets and Instagram posts in early March, parsed without cease by the media as regret for leaving the Heat behind, and as a signal that everything and anything is now in play for LeBron, including taking his talents back to South Beach.

Bullshit. LeBron's problem is the Golden State Warriors. His problem is Steph Curry. His problem is the regular season is almost done, and the Cavs are still talking about sacrifice and sharing, and they're 49-20, but the Warriors, who opened the season by winning twenty-four straight games, and played into late January with Steve Kerr at home due to back surgery gone bad, are an unholy 62-7.

LeBron James knows that the '96 Bulls, led by the second-greatest player ever, finished 72-10, the best season in NBA history, and waltzed to a championship with thirty-two-year-old MJ averaging 27-5-4.

LeBron knows that after 69 games, that Chicago team, featuring none other than Steve Kerr as its sniper, was 61-8.

LeBron knows that Steph Curry is already the consensus MVP, that Steph Curry is the new face of the NBA, proof of God, and the greatest single force in the known universe, counting gravity.

And LeBron doesn't like it, any of it.

When the levee finally breaks, it's in where else but fucking Miami. The 122-101 trouncing is bad enough, but when the Cavs come out for the halftime shootaround, already down twenty-one, LeBron's laughing it up with Dwyane Wade by the Heat bench.

Lue calls out LeBron right after the game.

"I just told him we can't have that—being down like we were, and him being the leader. Just me being a competitor, I didn't like it. We had a long talk about it. He understood, he apologized—it was good."

Better than good: LeBron bears down, on and off the court, and in the locker room. "Zero Dark 23"—his coinage for his ritual shunning of all social media to get his mind right for the playoffs—starts now. He stops DJing after wins, and goes with headphones. He unfollows the Cavs' Twitter feed, leading to another roundelay among the media about his feelings and his future, then puts up a triple-double against Denver the same day, and the Cavs clinch the Central Division.

THE ESPN 30 FOR 30 *Believeland* premieres on March 31, at the Palace Theatre, a temple of vaudeville splendor—Carrara marble, crystal chandeliers, sweeping staircases—that dates back to 1922. Last time I was in the joint was the day after my bar mitzvah, in 1965; my father flew in from Los Angeles, showed up at shul, took me and my brother Dave to the Palace to see *Help!*, starring a then-hot four-piece Merseybeat combo called the Beatles, and flew back to Los Angeles.

The place looks fab. It seats 2,700, and it's sold out, and so many folks wanted tickets that they've added three more showings. Lisa and Judah stayed home, but I wouldn't miss this for the world. I've got a producer credit, but I haven't seen a second of film—I didn't want to. I do know that Andy

Billman, the director, used the stuff with Judah and me as a narrative frame for the thing, and I trust his judgment completely.

I've asked many actors over the years if they watch their own movies, and every one of them has said no, and I realize why as soon as I hear my voice and see myself at the Huron Square Deli. It's something like a nightmare: I'm watching and listening to myself, a big lout on a huge screen lecturing his son about LeBron and Cleveland sports.

We're back at the deli at the end, too. Judah tells me that he loves Cleveland. I pull him close and kiss his head. That's all I know. There's a lot of horrible Cleveland sports history in between, all of which I've already relived a thousand times, and it's all I can do to keep from fleeing into the night and back to New Jersey.

I have to stay because I'm on a panel after the film. My brain's still locked in horror, but I take my seat onstage. There's Andy and a couple of other media guys and two legends: Earnest Byner, author of The Fumble in the 1987 AFC Championship game against Denver, and Craig Ehlo, over whom Michael Jordan sank The Shot. All that's missing is José Mesa, the son-of-a-bitch closer who blew a one-run lead in the ninth inning of Game 7 of the '97 World Series, and my sainted mother.

Sad doesn't begin to cover what I'm feeling seeing Byner and Ehlo. It took me *YEARS* to get over my rage at Byner, and at Lenny Wilkens, the Cavs coach who stuck poor Craig Ehlo between Jordan and glory. We are gathered to celebrate our love and loyalty in the face of fifty years of communal failure and misery, and all I'm thinking about is what a ridiculous asshole I am, and how much better I'd feel typing and alone. This is not survivor's remorse. It's shame.

I see and hear myself more than enough at home; I don't need to watch the movie. Enough to know that it exists in the world, that I'm with my son, that we are part of the story, now and forever.

This was not my plan. It is my fate, to sit, immortal, the bottom-feeding fan badgering his kid, Cleveland sports misery made flesh, and plenty of it.

I'm no pariah anymore.

I. Am. Legend.

EVERYTHING'S JUST RIGHT GOING into the playoffs, especially King James. LeBron's averaging close to a triple-double since going Zero Dark 23. He's ready.

"My body feels great. To be able to still be bouncing the way I'm bouncing and jumping the way I'm jumping—I feel like I'm in my early twenties again. It's a great feeling."

Give Lue credit: the Cavs, chased by Toronto, don't clinch the top seed in the East until the second-to-last day of the season because Tyronn Lue's smart and experienced enough to give LeBron and Kyrie whole games off going down the stretch.

"I think health going into the playoffs is more important than the seeding," Lue says. "All championship teams have to win on the road anyway. I think being healthy going into the playoffs is more important."

Love and Irving are healed. Everyone's sharing nice. The Cavs are playing faster, shooting more threes, going small more often—Mozgov rarely plays at all—LeBron running point, Kyrie looking to attack, Love at the elbow, Tristan down low, JR spotting up. With the rock in LeBron's hands, it finds the right man.

The defense is still a question, but you can't defend that lineup. That lineup is good enough to win the NBA championship—in any other year but this.

Golden State finishes 73-9, the best regular-season record in NBA history. They're 40-1 at home. In 2015, Steph set a single-season record with 286 three-pointers; this season, he nails 402.

Kerr doesn't rest his guys. They want the Bulls' record, and they're young and healthy, and they get it on the final day of the season. Steph hits ten threes, scores forty-six in thirty minutes—What can I say? Why would any Cleveland fan my age be surprised by any of this? A city bereft of civic glory, never mind a fucking championship, for half a fucking century; a native son turns infidel and leaves as a—what's that word again? Oh yeah: "pariah"—and then he is back, a messiah. It is the greatest sports story ever told, in some other town.

NO EASTERN CONFERENCE TEAM is good enough to stop the Cavaliers. The Pistons are this year's Celtics: young and well coached, by Stan Van Gundy—rumpled, squat, potbellied, forever screaming, always hoarse, the image of our plumber— but without the Cavs' talent and experience. Like Boston, all Detroit can do to keep it close is rough it up.

The elbow throwing starts early and ends in a four-game sweep. LeBron is so pissed off at the Pistons' center Andre Drummond for a forearm bar to the neck—and at the league for not suspending him—that he stalks off the court after Game 4 without a hug or a handshake.

It's all good. Nobody gets hurt this time around, thank goodness. The Cavs don't turn the ball over; they don't stop raining threes; they're finding the open man, trusting each other, spacing the floor with shooters, freeing LeBron to attack the rim or dish off to a wide-open Irving, Love, JR, RJ, Delly, or Frye—Lue has built a solid second unit—for an unguarded three.

The offense is nearly perfect in its balance. Kyrie averages twenty-seven, LeBron twenty-three, Love twenty-one. And they're playing harder defense, switching quicker—Tristan's fast enough to show hard on guards at the three-point arc and get back to defend a big down low. Without having to carry so much of the offensive load for so many minutes, LeBron's locked in on defense.

It's gorgeous out there on the floor. Kyrie Irving hits 47 percent of his threes for the series. Kevin Love pounds the boards even when his shot's not falling. And LeBron is that he is and does what he does: Everything, on both ends. Every fucking thing.

Lue is the *emmes*, more than ready for his first playoff series as an NBA head coach. He moves Love to center, drawing Drummond out and opening the middle, and LeBron destroys the Pistons blitzing to the paint, and Kyrie and JR murder them with threes. Lue dreams up end-of-quarter trickeration and plays coming out of time-outs that end up buckets. After the Game 4's final buzzer, Van Gundy—who has coached *eighteen* playoff series and had Lue as a player with Orlando—hugs Lue and says he always knew Lue would make a great head coach.

"It means a lot," says Lue. "To beat Stan, and beat him 4-0, that means a lot to me. Because I know he's a bad motherfucker."

Tell them, T-Lue. Ball doesn't lie. Game knoweth game. *And beat him 4-0*: This I love. He isn't rubbing Stan Van's nose in it—he's just saying. Because Tyronn Lue is a bad motherfucker, too.

LAST SEASON, DAN GILBERT paid J. R. Smith $6.5 million to play basketball. The day after the Cavs sweep Detroit, the city of Cleveland settles the federal lawsuit brought by Tamir Rice's family. They'll get $6 million—$3 million now, $3 million next year—for the murder of their boy.

Tim McGinty, the county prosecutor who made certain the cops walked, and lost his reelection bid, offers no comment. Steve Loomis, the president of the Cleveland Police Patrolman's Association, in lieu of silence or human decency, offers advice to the bereaved.

"We can only hope the Rice family and their attorneys will use a portion of this settlement to help educate the youth of Cleveland in the dangers associated with the mishandling of both real and facsimile firearms."

I can't say I'm shocked. I can't say much of anything, and anything I say is filtered through the kind of privilege that enables me to worry for my son's safety in a world full of zip lines, drunks, and germs, but never give a nanoscecond's thought to what might happen if the wrong Glen Ridge police car pulls him over.

I'm okay with just typing his name, Tamir Rice, to remember and pay respect. It's legit martyrology. It happened on my watch and in my tribe. I'm a father. I'm a Clevelander. I'm a human being.

ALL BUT THE FAN part of me, which is subhuman, monstrous. I know this because when Steph Curry sprains the medial collateral ligament in his right knee after slipping on a damp spot on the court in Game 4 against the Rockets in Houston, I don't feel bad about it—but when it turns out to be only a grade one sprain, I do.

THE CAVS BITCH-SLAP THE Hawks in round two. I'm in town alone for the opening games. I've grown a beard, not for luck, but to avoid being recognized at the Q by anyone who saw *Believeland*. I stop at the Huron Square Deli to say hello and grab a bite to eat, but it's gone out of business. Four blocks from the Q, it's a ghost town.

At the Q, the influence of Herr Trump's post-Weimar rally stylings on Dan Gilbert has turned the fan experience full Fascist. We are ordered to sing the national anthem a cappella en masse. We are told to stand at the beginning of the first and third quarters, and to remain standing in place until the Cavs score. Each program holds a placard stating the LAWS OF THE LAND. The cameras shame those few who refuse to don their provided T-shirts, and when their images loom up on the Humongotron, das Volk boo. Fascism: what fun.

The Hawks don't wish to mix it up, and so the Cavs can relax and enjoy themselves. Game 1 is a romp; Game 2 is a festival: forty-five of the Cavs' eighty-seven shots are threes, and twenty-five of those are makes, more threes than any NBA team has ever sunk in one game, regular season or playoff, led by JR's seven.

"He's the only one on the team who has the ultra–green light," LeBron says after the carnage subsides. "It's like fluorescent. Coach says, 'Hey, JR, shoot! Shoot it, shoot it, shoot it.'"

It's 74-38 at the half, 123-98 by the end, and the only Hawk willing to show up for the mandated postgame presser is a backup center who spent fourteen minutes on the court, gazing upward at the rainbows. No team has ever been more ready for eighteen holes of golf than these Atlanta Hawks against the Cleveland Cavaliers.

"We're making the right play," Lue says. "Kevin posts up, they double-team, we make the right pass out of the double

team: swing, swing, shot. Or they double-team LeBron in
the post—or we drive in transition—LeBron's driving seams,
Kyrie's driving seams, and guys are open. And if we're open,
we want to shoot those shots."

It's no fun alone, me and my beard, no fun at the game
and no fun on the haul back to North Jersey. Before hitting
the road, I take my customary leak next to the hybrid; two
guys walk past, cackling at the dribble of my mighty sword.

Yo, I got a note from the urologist.

"What's it say?"

It says ANY OTHER YEAR. It says Steph Curry came back
after missing four games and scored forty off the fucking
bench, including seventeen in overtime, an NBA record, and
the Warriors are rolling. It says only in Cleveland.

15

HALLELUJAH

The farm animals posing as humans at the Q are booing "O Canada" and I'm not blaming Donald Trump, who is merely the product of this nation's sick soul. First of all, then, I send love and respect to Toronto and the whole Dominion—our neighbor and true pal—and heartfelt thanks for Neil Young and G-d bless Leonard Cohen.

We good? Good. Then you won't hold it against me when I say that your Raptors are a dry hors d'oeuvre, barely worth the gas and the screaming of the deer. Give them credit for their two victories in Toronto, but the Cavs take their four wins by an average of nearly thirty points per game. So thanks for playing, *eh?*, and good luck with the Leafs: fifty years between crowns is an eternity, even in a minor sport.

The Cavs are healthy; they're playing great basketball; they have the best player on the floor each night. LeBron's attack is relentless—he finishes with more points and assists than any other player on either team, and more steals—and no one's talking about efficiency after he shoots 62 percent from the floor for the series. The team's balance and flow are ideal. Kyrie leads them in scoring in two of the wins, Love in a third, but when Game 6, the elimination game, comes, it's LeBron who peels off fourteen points in the first quarter, stealing all hope from these young Raptors. He winds up with thirty-three; Kyrie adds thirty, Love twenty, JR fifteen, and Cleveland moves on, on to heaven's gate, 113-87.

The Cavs are now 12-2 this postseason—and Game 6 is LeBron's first thirty-point game. He is fresh. They are ready.

"I know our city deserves it," LeBron says when it's done. "Our fans deserve it. But that gives us no sense of entitlement—we've still got to go out and get it."

He's heading to his sixth straight NBA Finals, the first non–Boston Celtic ever to do so. I've been a sports fan all my life, not just a Cleveland homer, and all in all, I've never disrespected a ring, not even Jeter's. But players don't win rings—teams do. And I've never seen a better athlete, on any team in any sport, than LeBron James.

STEPH'S UNANIMOUS MVP TROPHY—the media votes before the playoffs begin—is presented the day after his forty-pointer against Portland.

"I never really set out to change the game," says Steph. "What I wanted to do was be myself."

Kawhi Leonard gets fifty-four second-place votes to LeBron's forty, which has to be a joke, unless he gets points for not messing with his own team on social media.

Curry isn't just another pretty face. He IS efficiency, the first NBA player to average thirty a game in less than thirty-five minutes. He is the only player to shoot at least 50 percent from the floor, 45 percent from three, and 90 percent on free throws since a pair of white guys named Steve—Nash and Kerr.

LeBron does not begrudge it. Much. Out loud, anyway.

"Look at Steph's numbers," King James says. "Do you have any debate over that, really, when it comes to the award? So take nothing away from him—but when you talk about 'most valuable,' you can have a different conversation."

TRUE THAT. IT BEGINS on June 2, in Oakland, after Oklahoma City blows a three-games-to-one lead in the Western Conference Finals in a wild series that features Draymond Green kneeing the scrotum of the Thunder's seven-foot New Zealander, Steven Adams, in Game 3. It's Green's third flagrant of the playoffs, and the second time in two games he's buried a leg in Adams's junk, but the league refuses to suspend him. They fine Green instead, with the league's dean of discipline explaining to a snickering sports world that "during a game, players—at times—flail their legs in an attempt to draw a foul."

Green's presence in Game 4 is no help: he has six points and six turnovers, Curry misses eight of ten threes, and OKC wins. One more Thunder win and the Warriors' season is over, and the Cavs would have home court in the Finals against a Thunder team they've beaten both games they played this year. This would be more than okay with me.

Nope. We're talking about Cleveland sports here. The Warriors take Game 7, and roar into the Finals as the tenth team in NBA history to come back to win a playoff series after being down 3-1.

"No one ever had any doubt that we could get this done," Draymond says. "People have seen teams down 3-1 before, but they ain't seen many—they've definitely never seen a 73-win team down 3-1."

There's a lot to like about Dray. Saginaw kid, four full years playing for Izzo at Michigan State, donated $3 million to MSU. When he arrived in the NBA and saw how much it costs to live in San Francisco, he found an apartment in Emeryville, just outside Oakland, to save on rent.

"I've been pretty broke my entire life," Green said. "I'm not going to live that same life, but I'm going to keep those same principles."

They say Draymond has a chip on his shoulder because he didn't go in the first round, that he has memorized the names of all thirty-four players taken before him in the 2012 draft, and now he's an NBA champion and All-Star, kicking opponents in the balls.

They say that he's the heart and soul of Golden State, but I prefer Joe Lacob, their venture-capitalist majority owner, who got blown at call-your-doctor length by the *New York Times Magazine* when the Warriors were still en route to win number seventy-three.

"The great, great venture capitalists who built company after company," Lacob says, "that's not an accident. And none of this is an accident, either. We're light-years ahead of probably every other team, in structure, in planning, in how we're going to go about things. We've crushed them on the basketball court, and we're going to, for years, because of the way we've built this team."

Fuck you, pally. I'm not a venture capitalist, but I do know Jewbris when I hear it. Go ahead, landsman, dare the gods. No man is author of his fate. The only question is whether a venture capitalist is in fact a man.

Las Vegas says the Warriors are six-point favorites for Game 1 and –210 for the series—heavy, heavy favorites. I might take some of that action if I were a venture capitalist, or a gentile, or a fan of any other city's teams.

Maybe just a grand, for the sake of the book?

"No," Judah says.

Not the 529 money, I swear.

"No."

Wait. I'll put it on the Dubs. Win-win. Genius.

"No."

THE HOUSE IS NERVOUS. I'm a mess. Men from the shul— kind and gentle men, friends who helped with our son's bar mitzvah—ask to join us to watch.

No.

This is not fun and games. This is my entire bucket list. I

have lived large. I slept at Bill Murray's house, smoked a joint with Tupac, ate blintzes with Paul Giamatti. I have a loving wife on whose fecund womanhood my seed found purchase, and two toilets. You are not welcome in my home. I cannot pretend to be human while another Cleveland team takes a dump on my dreams.

"Enjoy every moment," LeBron tells his team in their pre-game huddle. "Every second. Every play."

But these are not the good Cavs; it is uphill from the start, and the Cavs are down fourteen and bricking bunnies in the paint, late on D, sloppy with the ball. JR looks like he doesn't want to shoot, a look no one has ever seen before this game.

Busy spraying oaths and spittle on the dog, I don't notice when Lisa goes upstairs to take off her JR T-shirt. I'm guessing it's early in the third quarter, before the Cavs rally back and Kerr calls a time-out, smashing his plastic clipboard, breaking it in two while he screams at his team, after which the Warriors go on a fifteen-point run, icing the game, winning 104-89.

Odd: Curry and Klay score only twenty points combined, and Draymond sixteen. The Cavs get beat by Leandro Barbosa and Shaun Livingston, coming off the bench for Kerr. The Cavaliers play tight—from LeBron on down the line.

"When you're outscored forty-five to ten in bench points and give up twenty-five points off turnovers," LeBron says afterward, "you're not winning that game."

The only highlight comes when Delly whacks Iggy in the groin near the end of the third. Nothing flagrant—a starter's pistol going off, an ungentle reminder that every man jack out there totes a sack of jewelry, dangling just behind his shorts.

Iggy, woke, nails a long three after the nutshot. And another. A pair.

"How'd it go?" Lisa asks when finally I trudge upstairs.

They lost by fifteen. JR scored three more points than you did.

"What's wrong with them?"

I don't know. I do not know.

It's Cleveland sports. Of all the wrong things I don't know how to fix, I don't know this the most.

GAME 2 IS SUNDAY and it is worse. Much worse. Worse than the 132-98 embarrassment that greased Blatt's skis. The final score is 110-77, and it wasn't that close. No one can buy a three. LeBron turns it over seven times. Barbosa and Livingston outscore Kyrie and JR, 17-15. Draymond Green leads Golden State with twenty-eight points, to LeBron's nineteen.

Two of Green's total come on a layup over Love, who's writhing on the floor after getting hit in the back of the head by an inadvertent Harrison Barnes elbow, which is advertently attached to Harrison Barnes. After he scores, Draymond turns to face Love, still on the floor, and, with nobody nearby to kick, flexes his biceps.

Love is concussed, and will likely miss Game 3. As if it

matters. The Cavs have now lost seven straight games to Golden State, including the first two games of this Finals by a combined forty-eight points. Thirty-two teams in Finals history have been down two games to none. Three have come back.

"It's hard for me to kind of pinpoint what's not working and what could work right now," says LeBron. "Obviously, not much is working. We gotta bear down."

Coach Lue seems unfazed. Not happy, no. But calm. Matter-of-fact, as always.

"They were tougher than us, and more aggressive. They took care of home court—we know we're going home. The guys are not discouraged. More pissed than anything. We've got to be tougher."

The only question to belabor here in Glen Ridge is whether one would choose to get swept rather than heartbroken in a Game 7.

Lisa's preference is the heartbreak. Not me. I've lived through both. Better to get it over with and prep for next year's nightmare. She's from upstate New York—she still sometimes forgets to lock the doors. I'm from Cleveland, where nothing is given and nothing is promised and nothing is precisely what's delivered.

Cleveland *is* life: you do the best you can with what you've got, keep working on your game, stay healthy, get a little luck, and at the end of the road trip—nothingness.

That's why we need myth, of course. You call yours God. I call mine Jim Brown.

GOOD NEWS! AFTER INTERVIEWING with the New York Knicks, the Houston Rockets, and the Sacramento Kings, all seeking a fresh start with a new head coach, David Blatt signs on to lead Darussafaka, bulwark of the Turkish Basketball Super League. He'll be coaching EuroLeaguers in Istanbul, where Volkswagen Arena seats 5,240 fans.

"I think I did enough good things in the NBA, and I know enough people, to where if it's my desire in some way, shape, or form to come back, that I could. But I'm trying to focus right now on my next challenge."

I don't know if he went on to ask the Turks if anyone recalled Steve Jobs's last words. I'm guessing not.

GADZOOKS! THE CAVS ARE favored by one point for Game 3 at the Q. And Golden State's –1000 for the Finals now, the Cavs +650. A grand on the Cavs pays $6,500.

"No. That's insane."

Psalm 19, bub: *"There is no speech nor language, where their voice is not heard / Their line is gone out through all the earth, and their words to the end of the world."*

"What does that even mean?"

You put your faith where your mouth is. Faith, money, I don't know. Verses three and four.

"How does it end?"

"Let the words of my mouth, and the meditation of my heart, be acceptable in thy sight, O Lord, my strength and my redeemer.

Back when I sang it in shul, it was my *rock*, not *redeemer*. This is the King James Version. *King James.*

"No."

He's right. Burning cash is Sandy's thing, not mine—*WAS* Sandy's thing: my brother Michael texts me Wednesday morning, the morning of Game 3, that Sanford Raab just threw his last seven.

I'LL SAY THIS MUCH for my father, and more about myself in saying so: His absence inspired me. His absence didn't loom over my life—his absence WAS my life. I was no more inclined to see or speak with him in hospice than he was to show up when I needed him as a boy. I saw him last late in 2013, when I was in LA to profile Danny DeVito—not the peak of my magazine career—and all he did was complain about my brother and his wife, the only people left who cared.

I'm not flying to Los Angeles, and I'm not driving to Cleveland, either. The kid—my son—is running the second leg of the 4×800 tonight in Berkeley Township.

I catch up with him before his heat.

You're running your leg for Grampa Sandy.

"He died?"

He died. I'm sorry, bub. You're down to one grandparent.

"I'm sorry, too."

Like his mother, he's impossible to read. The last time he

saw Sandy was in 2012, and Sandy shit his sweatpants at the Du-par's on Ventura Boulevard and, without a word, carried his pantload—Welsh rarebit—into my rental and back to the Inn on Ventura, his old-age home back then. We walked behind him down the hall—my wife, my son, and me—smelling loose stool with every step.

You might think it cruel of me, this story, but you don't know Sandy Raab, didn't follow his foul trail. He knew he'd crapped down his leg, and when we got to his apartment, he went straight for the bathroom to wash up.

The bathroom door was cracked, and the smell of him, released in full, was stunning. You could taste the fucking rarebit.

Judah and I started laughing so hard it hurt.

Out he comes, wrapped in towels. Smirking.

"I had an accident," he says. "And you didn't even know it."

Alev ha-shalom, old man.

THE KID RUNS A 51.34 split, which won't get him into Princeton, but the Cavs annihilate the Warriors, 120-90. I'm watching on my cell at the meet, which, while miraculous to me—it wasn't so many years ago that I bought an AM antenna while I was living outside Philly, so I could maybe listen to Cleveland teams lose on the radio—is not optimal. Kyrie steps up, Jefferson steps in for Love, which improves the defense, at least on a two-inch screen, and JR locates his three-point shot, and LeBron is finally LeBron—thirty-two points, eleven boards.

The game's over by the time we get home, so I look for the postgame pressers on NBA.tv, and there's Jim Brown, sitting at a table set up on the floor of the Q, with Charles Barkley, Grant Hill, Steve Smith, and the obligatory white guy host.

The screen shows a photo of the 1967 Ali Summit, here in Cleveland, and Barkley asks JB—"Mister Brown," Chuck calls him—about the summit's greatest civil rights accomplishment.

"To stand up and be men. Be great Americans. Fight for our rights. Risk making all of the money, and the popularity—all we wanted was freedom, equality, and justice, like everybody else."

Of course: Muhammad Ali died five days ago, and the next day was the summit anniversary.

JB's sitting on the edge of a chair too tall for a bent old man, wearing a dark tracksuit. His fist around the microphone is beefy—bigger than Sir Charles's—his voice low, slow, and steady.

"We called out to the great athletes in the country. They all responded. They didn't ask for any airfare. They didn't ask for any rooms or anything like that. They were risking their careers."

Silence.

Then Steve Smith asks Brown about LeBron—"a modern-day hero"—as an athlete and man.

"He carries a heavy load," Brown says. "He has a generous

heart, and he works with charities. What I want to see him do is become an activist, and use all of that power and some of that money, and rally you guys so that you are forced—so that we can save some of these lives. The real deal is saving lives.

"You all have the resources and the influence—and if you go out there, and I know where to go, these young men can be turned around. You have the influence. You have the money. You have the intelligence. You're great Americans. You are successful. And those individuals out there have no fathers— they have nobody to truly look up to. So they look up to each other. They don't mind dying. They don't mind killing."

Strong enough? God *DAMN.* Jim Brown has spent forty years in inner cities and prisons, trying. Long ago, he gave up whatever hope he may have had that White America would ever come to its senses or its soul and end the Civil War. No truly equal rights, no justice, no freedom, and surely no reparations, just casinos for the natives, and jail cells for the heirs of slavery, and choke holds, and bullets.

THE GAME ITSELF IS sweet, especially Kyrie, who explodes for sixteen in the first quarter. But there's a moment in the second half more precious than gold. With eleven seconds left in the third quarter and the Cavs up by nineteen, Shaun Livingston draws a shooting foul on Shumpert, who blocked his jumper but fouled him with his body. The whistle blows, the play is dead, but the ball launched by Livingston is still up in the air, and it bounces, once, high off the wood, and Steph

Curry darts forward, grabbing it with both hands, rising to the hoop as the players on both teams relax with the whistle.

LeBron's walking right under the hoop. He sees Curry grab the ball and go up for the layin, and, jumping straight up as Steph rises, LeBron nails the ball against the glass, swiping it away with his right hand—all this from a standstill.

LeBron and Steph exchange brief unpleasantries, and their teammates mill about, unaware of exactly what's going on. Nothing. Nothing at all. But something happens on Curry's dead-ball drive—something's revealed in LeBron's sudden move, and the dark glare that follows.

"I didn't want him to see it go in," LeBron explains after the game.

Simple enough. The truth is still out there on the floor and on tape: LeBron punks Curry, and Steph knows it. It's just one win, just one shining moment that means nothing on the scoreboard, but the Cavs are going to turn this shit around, and we're all going to Cleveland for Game 4.

GAME 4 GOES TO hell in the fourth quarter with the game tied at eighty-one. The Cavs go ice cold, scoreless for six and a half minutes, the Warriors start hitting threes, and at one point I look over at Judah sitting on the other side of Lisa, as he grabs the front of his freebie T-shirt at the neck and rips it open down his chest.

Such a proud moment. The cords in his neck are bulging. He's crimson. What a job I've done.

And what a fine idea this was. Twenty-six hundred bucks for three seats, a thousand more miles on the hybrid, the room at the Marriott, and all Judah gets is a cheap rag of a T-shirt and a 108-97 defeat. He's making his bones as a Cleveland sports fan, and it isn't pretty. I know.

Lisa's seething, too, quietly. JR cans only two of eight threes; Curry hits seven of his own—the Warriors hit seventeen threes, a Finals record—and Lisa's not a Steph fan. It's mostly the time she has spent watching constant TV close-ups of Curry tongue-fucking his plastic mouthguard.

"Look at that asshole."

That's the new face of the NBA.

"He's a child. *Look* at him."

I can tell that she's dehydrated, too—never a good thing. They won't let her bring water into the Q, and she won't pay Dan Gilbert's predatory prices, and I can't recall having a worse time at a sporting event, ever.

Once the game gets ugly—it's been chippy all along, with LeBron's getting pounded at the rim time after time without a foul call—it's nasty all over the court. With under three minutes to play and the Cavs down ten, Draymond and LeBron are tangling arms at center court as Green tries to set a screen for Curry, and Dray gets knocked to the floor—or flops.

I can't tell what happens next until they show it on the Humongotron—LeBron high-steps over Green, and Green bolts up and catches LeBron between his legs just as he passes over, with a quick backhand to his nuts, whereupon LeBron turns back in fury and they're tangling again, jawing at each other all the way to the basket with the ball still in play, until finally a ref blows his whistle, and their teammates step in to separate them.

The zebras confer and call a double foul—not even a tech on Green. They understand that after the hurting Green put on Steven Adams's sack, a technical or flagrant foul would trigger a suspension, and they'd prefer to let the league's front office make that call.

After the game, LeBron seems more upset about Dray calling him a bitch, though he won't use the word.

"I'm all cool with the competition, but some of the words that came out of his mouth were a little bit overboard. Being a guy with pride, a guy with three kids and a family, things of that nature, some things just go overboard, and that's where he took it."

I can't recall hearing any other pro athlete complain about name-calling before. Maybe pride and a semblance of dignity is all that's left. Tonight his line is 25-13-9, and Kyrie goes for thirty-four, and Love comes back off the bench and looks like Kevin Love, including iffy switching on D, and perhaps the time has come to surrender to reality: the Warriors are better than the Cavaliers. No one needs to remind LeBron that in the course of Finals history, thirty-two teams have gone down three games to one before tonight. Two of them— the 1951 Knicks and the 1966 Lakers—managed to force a Game 7. Both of them lost.

"Let's get one," LeBron says. "We've already got to take a

flight home anyways, so we might as well come home with a win and play on our home floor again."

Tyronn Lue's upset because LeBron spends forty-six minutes driving to the hoop and only gets to the foul line four times. League rules forbid coaches and players from critiquing officials in the media—"I'm going to save my twenty-five K," LeBron says when asked in the postgame presser about the refs tonight—but the Cavs coach speaks his mind.

"He never gets calls," Lue says. "He attacks the paint every single play, and he doesn't get a fair whistle because of his strength and power—guys bounce off him. But those are still fouls."

Me, I stopped whining about bad calls after the 1995 World Series, when the umps gave Maddux and Glavine a strike zone the size of Utah. Those aren't fouls if they don't get called, and there's nothing that a Cleveland fan can do but shut the fuck up and move on to the terminal stage— Game 5 in Oakland, Monday night.

"If you don't think you can win," says Lue, "don't get on the plane."

Go get 'em, Coach. Safe travel. I'll be watching from North Jersey, not rocking, not kicking the dog, just waiting for next year again.

ON SUNDAY, THE LEAGUE decides enough is enough. The dean of discipline has watched tape of Green flailing his legs into opposing crotches all season—Draymond kicks dicks on rebounds, too—and these aren't the stones of some musta-chioed lug from New Zealand we're talking about anymore.

We're talking about the King's jewels now. Draymond Green's suspended for Game 5. He's gone. LeBron's assessed a technical foul for taunting-by-step-over. He'll play.

T-Lue, fined the standard twenty-five large for complaining about the refs, revisits the day Allen Iverson stepped over him in the Finals.

"I didn't make a big deal out of it," Lue says. "After the game, it was a big deal and everybody was talking about it. But at the end of the day, we won. That's all that matters to me."

GREEN'S SUSPENSION IS FABULOUS news all by itself, but the way the Warriors react to it, and to LeBron, is every bit as welcome.

"I guess his feelings just got hurt," Klay Thompson says. "Guys talk trash in this league all the time—it's a man's league and I've heard a lot of bad things on that court. But at the end of the day, it stays on the court."

LeBron laughs and laughs when he's told about Klay's comments.

"I'm not going to comment because I know where it can go from this," James says. "It's hard to take the high road. I've been doing it for thirteen years. It's hard to continue to do it—and I'm going to do it again."

Not Golden State. Marreese Speights, the backup center

best known as Mo' Buckets, tweets a baby bottle emoji, and then Ayesha Curry, Steph's wife, cookbook author, Food Network star, model, and actress, tweets her opinion of the contretemps.

"High Road. Invisible bridge used to step over said person when open floor is available left to right."

I don't know if Ayesha's dehydrated or Speights and Klay are stupid, but this stuff is choice, a gift to all of Cleveland. The thirty-two NBA teams down three games to one in the Finals didn't have King James on the floor in Game 5, enraged.

LeBron blocks Curry from behind on a layup early in the first quarter, posterizes Speights, and finishes the first half with twenty-five points. Kyrie's having a great time taking Curry and Thompson to school off his dribble, faking past them to the basket, pulling up and stepping back for a three; with Green out and Andrew Bogut, the Warriors' starting center, sitting with a sprained knee, Kyrie gets it all. Golden State stays close. Klay Thompson's on fire, but Ayesha's hubby can't buy a shot, and tonight it's the Warriors going cold in the fourth and the Cavs step on their throats, and most of me can't believe what I'm seeing. I'm afraid to believe it.

LeBron and Kyrie each finish with forty-one, the first teammates in NBA history to ever score forty or more in a Finals game, but that's not what scares me. What scares me is a moment toward game's end when LeBron, falling backward, hits yet another shot, and Kyrie, rushing over before he can rise, bends over LeBron, his fists clenched, his eyes wide, screaming excitement and joy.

THIS terrifies me. These guys believe that they're going to win the championship. They believe they're going to be the first team in history to rise from the grave by winning three straight Finals games against the greatest NBA team of all time.

I can't begin to imagine it without feeling the ache I've felt since 1964. You don't get inured to it. Byner's fumble in 1988 hurt worse than Elway's 1987 drive. They still hurt—ALL of them—and here we go again, once more unto the breach.

"We're just happy we get another day," LeBron says. "That's all we can ask for—we got another day to survive."

Is it too late to say that I love this man?

GAME 6 IS IN Cleveland on Thursday night, and Judah has an honors breakfast that day, and a final exam in precalc on Friday morning, so it's good that he passed his driving test yesterday—his seventeenth birthday. He's solid behind the wheel, and the weather is good, so he handles the first leg while I sweat bullets in the passenger seat. Not that I don't trust him—I do. It's everyone else on I-80 I fear, plus the deer.

I need to piss.

"Again?"

There's a rest area at 194. It's urgent or I wouldn't ask.

We're passing 199, Mile Run: NO SERVICES.

"You'd think there'd at least be a gas station there."

Nothing. Don't even think about it, son. There's nothing there.

THE CROWD'S INSANE. Our a cappella "Banner" is strong. For all the bathos and boredom, and the miserable ending, life is good. Win or lose, it's wonderful. Win or lose, Judah, swift, strong, smiling, stands beside me. Life is . . . feh.

Writing about fatherhood is even worse than writing about sex. Every jackass is the world's first father, every writer writes about his own dad, kid, or both, and everyone's dog dies. Fine. Okay. It's what I do, what I've always done. Writing is who I've always been.

But this—life—is so much better, here, now, this moment, flames trumpeting from Dan's moronic scoreboard and the ceaseless howling of the Crump. Fuck Princeton and the future.

THIS.

Win or lose, we have this.

And this, too, I owe to LeBron James.

IT'S CLEAR FROM THE tip that the Cavs have eaten the Warriors' hearts. Draymond's back, Bogut's out with the knee, Iggy's in: it's Steve Kerr's vaunted Lineup of Death, tight, frightened, and falling back in wonderment as the lightning crashes down on them. Kyrie pulls up on Curry for the opening deuce, but only after the ball finds four different Cavs. At the other end, LeBron jabs the ball away from Klay, then streaks down the side for a return pass, Curry chasing him behind, helpless as LeBron slams it home.

Steph ain't sniffing Champagne now; he's smelling King James's ass. On the Cavs' next possession, Curry's on LeBron after a switch, and LeBron posts him like a schoolboy, laying it in. Next, Kyrie nails a three, and—after the first Warriors basket—he pushes hard to the rim, dishes it off, no-look, to LeBron flashing in him from the sideline; again he throws the hammer down.

It's 13-2.

It's the loudest crowd I've ever heard. By quarter's end, the Cavs are up twenty, 31-11—Golden State's lowest-scoring quarter of the season. Instead of getting back to defend after misses, they whine to the referees. Curry's out of sorts on both ends; Kerr pulls him halfway through the quarter, with three points and two fouls.

Curry and Klay heat up after halftime, but LeBron's laying waste tonight. He scores or assists on twenty-seven Cavs points in one third-to-fourth stretch, blocking Draymond at the rim for good measure. He is unstoppable, invincible. He is King James.

LeBron came back for *this*, and saw it slip away last June, on his home court, to these high-yellow heirs of NBA millionaires, who grew up in mansions on Easy Way. Call all this the raving of an aging, racist Jew, but when James blocks Curry from behind at the rim, just smacks the ball clean out of Steph's hands, he turns on Curry, snarling something as the ball bounces out of bounds.

On the Humongotron, the epithet seems to begin "chump-ass," but I can't be certain and Judah isn't sure, either, and I'd hate to get it wrong.

Ten seconds later, Curry, going for the steal, undercuts LeBron just as he turns upcourt with a rebound, Steph slaps him on the arm, commits a foul, and draws the whistle. Lue's clapping on the sideline; we're all going apeshit, because this is Steph Curry's sixth personal: he is disqualified from further play tonight.

The new face of the NBA flings his ravished mouthguard, useless now, into the first row of courtside fans, and we wave him good-bye all the way to the tunnel, baying "ASSHOLE" in unison.

The final score is 115-101. LeBron gets another forty-one, with seventeen in the fourth quarter, eleven assists, eight rebounds, four steals, three blocks, and one turnover. In forty-three minutes of jackhammer power and a touch of efficiency.

But please, tell me more about Michael and the *SIX RINGZZZ*, and Kobe, too, of course, those abusive, sociopathic winners.

And I'll tell you that if I'm an NBA GM choosing one of these three, in their primes or at age thirty-one, to stake my team on, I'll take LeBron.

Teams win rings.

THE KID HAS TO get back for the test, so he studies while I drive. We're flying back Sunday morning, Father's Day, on ESPN's dime: Andy Billman's hoping to put another, happier ending on *Believeland*, so he needs to shoot us watching Game 7.

The whole thing feels weird. Game 7 with the kid, in Cleveland on Father's Day with Sanford Raab's ashes still cooling down. I must give LeBron the dime here, but the hockey assist goes to Sandy Raab.

I have more room in my heart for him, now that he's dead—whatever that says about me.

It all feels all right, right now, riding with my son.

He's asleep by Dubois, God love him. No problem. I may be old, but I can still drive the lane all night.

THE GOLDEN STATE WARRIORS are a mess, starting with Steve Kerr.

"He gets six fouls called on him, and three of them were absolutely ridiculous. The MVP of the league, and we're talking about touch fouls in the NBA Finals. I'm happy he threw his mouthpiece."

Me too, Coach. I'm also happy you brought up the whole MVP thing. Thank you. Klay calling Bron a snitch, Dray calling him a bitch, Mo's baby bottle, sweet Ayesha's tweets: those things matter much less to LeBron James than being the league's most valuable player.

NO TEAM EVER HAS come back from being down three games to one to win an NBA Championship.

The home team won fifteen of the last eighteen Finals Game 7s.

The home team has won the last six Finals Game 7s.

The last road team to win a Game 7 was the Washington Bullets—now the Wizards—in 1978.

"I'll play it anywhere," LeBron says. "It's two of the greatest words in the world—'Game Seven.' Let's just go out and play and see what happens. I can't wait."

SLUDGY OUT THERE. This is Golden State's 106th game this season. Thanks to the early round sweeps, the Cavs have played three fewer. Throw in Finals travel and the pressure of Game 7, and it isn't beautiful basketball. It's a war of attrition.

LeBron sees this, knows this going in. Lue knows it, too, as does Kerr. Both teams are fatigued, banged up, but the basic truths remain: Cleveland can't run and shoot with Golden State, and LeBron James is the best basketball player ever born of woman.

Eighty-two points in the last two games don't matter tonight. Tonight LeBron's passing first, and the ball is moving, and within the first five minutes, all five Cavs have scored. Love's pounding glass on both ends. Kyrie's shot isn't there, but he's finding his spots and he's playing Steph hard on defense.

Golden State's hitting threes—Dray's on fire—and they're

trying to up the pace, but LeBron's bringing it up slow after almost every Warrior bucket, burning clock, limiting Warriors' possessions, running the half-court offense, probing and passing. He sees Green on JR beyond the arc and fires a laser to him. JR fakes the shot and drives by Green for an easy deuce, and at the end of one, it's 23-22 Golden State.

The Cavs can't buy a three, but they don't get rattled. They're hustling back on defense, calling the right switches, Love is showing hard on pick and rolls and getting back to his man. Draymond's four for four on threes; by the middle of the second, LeBron has ten—he's going hard to the rim— with eight rebounds and five assists. And with five minutes to go in the half and the Cavs down two, he blocks Steph Curry going to the rim again, and they bump chests.

Curry's chirping. LeBron doesn't even look at him.

As the half winds down, though, so do the Cavaliers. Golden State has hit nine of nineteen threes, the Cavs one of twelve. The only thing going for Kyrie are the Uncle Drew angles off the glass. The defense stays mainly solid, but Green's open at the top of the arc over and over, and he isn't missing—he has twenty-two points by halftime, with six rebounds and five assists.

LeBron has twelve, eight, and five.

The Cavs are down 49-42.

IT FEELS LIKE TWENTY points down to me. We're in the Wild Eagle Saloon, in downtown Cleveland, with a fucking film crew shooting us watching the game with three, four hundred drunken Clevelanders. The kid's loving it—he's a pop star now, thanks to *Believeland*; people stop us on the street for handshakes and selfies. I am not author of my fate, or the kid's, but, for one night at least, I am the world's greatest father.

Draymond finally misses, and JR nails a two, and Tristan, of all people, takes a pass from LeBron to the hole for another two points, and two LeBron lasers find JR and JR swishes them both and it's tied at fifty-four.

The Cavs are playing harder now—harder than the Warriors. I'm glad they pushed hard for their seventy-three wins, glad that Lue rested his stars en route to the playoffs. LeBron's running clock and dishing, Love has eleven rebounds already, and Kyrie's driving, juking, and stutter-stepping, blurring by Draymond, snatching a steal, going the length of the floor, and finishing with a left-handed lob that just grazes the top of glass and, spent, plops right in.

Kerr calls time-out with the Cavs up 65-59 after an 11-0 run. I'm not counting any chickens here, but Kyrie has twenty-one points with twelve in the third. This could happen. This is happening.

Give the Warriors full credit. Kerr goes smaller, Draymond hits yet another three, and Golden State fights back to tie it at seventy-one. The Cavs look exhausted. They're down a point going into the fourth.

I shrug at the kid. He shrugs back. It's too loud to hear, and what is there to say?

Golden State's tired, too.
We've got LeBron.
It's Cleveland.
This can't end well.

LEBRON GETS THE FIRST points of the fourth on a return pass from Love. LeBron's running again. Love's running. Love hits a short hook off a pass from LeBron, Klay klanks a trey, Jefferson finds Kyrie, who misses from two feet, then darts past Draymond, grabs the rebound, falls back, launching it off the glass and into the basket.

Time-out, Golden State.

81-78 Cavs.

LeBron counters a Green make with a running one-hander, but Curry hits a three, JR misses, and Klay and Green hit.

The Warriors are up 87-83.

LeBron finds seven-foot Festus Ezeli out beyond the arc on a horrible Warriors switch, draws the foul, and sinks all three. 87-86.

On the Warriors' next possession, Steph tries to go behind his back with a pass meant for Klay and throws it out of bounds. Call it stupidity. Call it fatigue. Either way, it's the Cavs' ball, and LeBron walks it up slow and nails a three from twenty-six feet. Dray finds Klay on a drive and he scores.

89-89. 4:39 left to go. Both teams are deadened now, missing everything. And then, with 1:55 left, Kyrie misses from in close, the ball comes out to Iguodala, and he's sprinting down the court, Steph trailing on the wing—and only J. R. Smith stands between the two of them and the rim.

Iguodala passes to Curry on the run, and Steph sends it back to Iggy, and JR lays back, afraid to foul, and up goes Iguodala, and from nowhere on the Wild Eagle screen, LeBron comes skying, soaring as the ball leaves Iguodala's hands, and he blocks the fucking shot.

If I live a thousand years, I will never see a better play or a better basketball player. Build the motherfucking statue. That's the legacy. That's the greatest thing my eyes have ever seen—that and this kid in my arms.

ACKNOWLEDGMENTS

For their insight, guidance, and friendship, thanks to Bryan Bracey, Sean Manning, Brian Spaeth, Alex Belth, Joe Posnanski, Ken Carman, Joe Gabriele, Jay Woodruff, Bob Ivry, Vince Grzegorek, Jack Sanders, Joey Blackstone, Bill Shapiro, Brian Abrams, Tom Reed, Bob Parsons, Michelle Herman, Pete Beatty, Ethan Skolnick, Peter Schmader, Rabbi Elliott Tepperman, landlord Brian Windhorst, Roldo Bartimole, and the sole hero of the Hundred Years' War, Tony Grossi.

Special thanks go to Dave Buynak, a special guy who never wavered in his faith or generosity.

My brothers—Dave, Bob, and Michael—joined me in Cleveland in August 2016, the first time in twenty-five years the four of us were in one place together. Michael brought some of Sandy's cremains, and we had a wonderful time when I needed them most. They helped me more than I can say in words.

My *Esquire* compadres are family forever. Junod, Chiarella, Pierce, Sager, Fussman, John H., Jones, Warren, Kenney, McCammon, Peele, Cabot, Griffin, Hintelmann, Curcurito, Zarinski, D'Agostino, Dorment: I owe all of you my gratitude, love, and respect.

That goes double for Granger, the best friend, editor, and prince any writer ever loved.

David Hirshey and Barry Harbaugh edited *The Whore of Akron*, and when they moved on left me in Luke Dempsey's gentile hands. I got lucky with all three. Hirshey came up with *You're Welcome, Cleveland* as a title in 2014, and he and Harbaugh went through the Cavs' loss in the 2015 Finals along with me. Luke inherited me down 0-2 to the Warriors last year, and his confidence and clarity meant the world to me, and, apparently, to the Cavaliers.

David Black is much more than a great friend and literary agent. He's one tough, inspiring motherfucker. Without that man in my corner, I don't know how I'd do what I do.

Reed Bergman is my friend and broadcast agent. All you need to know about RB is that he's from Cleveland and he got me a shot at ESPN. He is a wizard, and deserves an NFL team far better than the Cleveland Browns. Someday, brother. Some distant day.

I'm grateful to ESPN for giving me a taste of TV glory. Special thanks to Rob King, Jack Obringer, and Rob Savatelli, and to Jeremy Schaap, Wright Thompson, Don Van Natta Jr., and Jay Crawford.

Thanks also to ESPN Films and John Dahl for supporting *Believeland*; to Gary Cohen, who brought me aboard; and to the incredible Andy Billman, my soul brother, who got it done and made it great.

My family in Cleveland is the Elinsky tribe, beginning with Howard, Ken, and Sharon, friends of more than fifty years, and extending to their spouses, kids, and cousins. Their loving kindness and support is the best part of my commute to Cuyahoga County.

I fell madly in love with Lisa Brennan in 1993. The planet shook, my life changed forever, and I am still madly in love with Lisa Brennan. I don't truly understand love or marriage, and that's okay. It's enough for me to love and be loved by Lisa Brennan. Lisa is my heart. Judah Raab is my soul. Thank you both for everything.

ABOUT THE AUTHOR

SCOTT RAAB is a graduate of Cleveland State University and the University of Iowa's Writers' Workshop. A native Clevelander, he now lives in Glen Ridge, New Jersey.